THE SISTERS STAY DROPPING GEMS!

What Women In The Bible Teach Us
About Life, Love, And Relationships

By

Kimberly Bulgin

Published by KIAB ENTERPRISES
First Edition, 2025

ISBN: 979-8-218-60230-7

Scripture Acknowledgment:
All Scripture quotations, unless otherwise indicated, are taken from the New King James Version® (NKJV®). Copyright © 1982 by Thomas Nelson. Used by permission. All rights reserved.

Disclaimer:
This is a work of nonfiction. The views expressed are those of the author and do not necessarily reflect the opinions of any organization, institution, or individual mentioned in the text.

For permissions or inquiries, please contact:
info@kimberlybulgin.com
www.kimberlybulgin.com

FOR DAD:

To the man who taught

me that a woman's place

is wherever God calls her

to be.

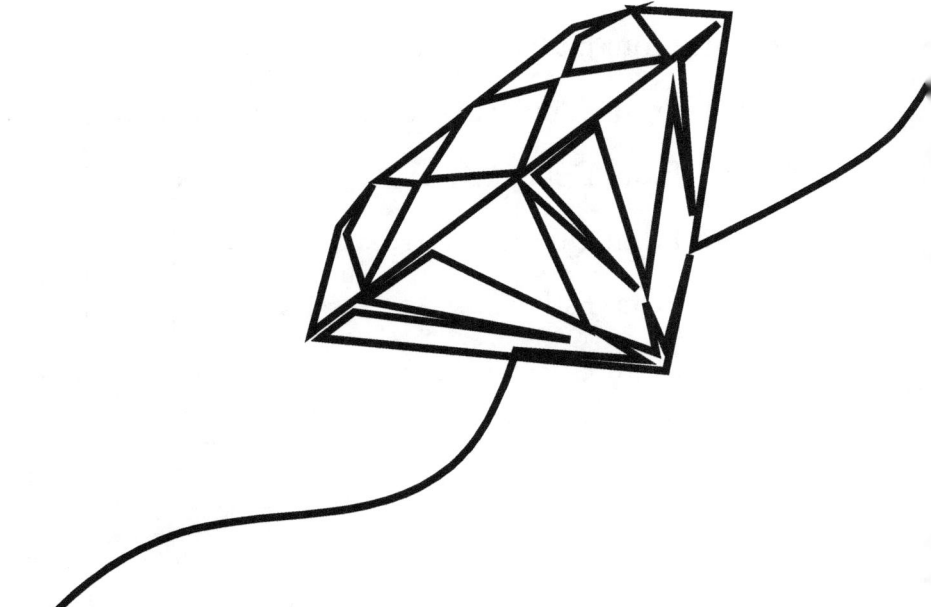

TABLE OF CONTENTS

WHY THIS BOOK AND
WHY YOU NEED IT NOW

Sometimes, I walk into a room, forget I'm wearing sunglasses, and wonder why everything looks so dark. When I finally take them off, it's as if I could burst into song: "I can see clearly now; the rain is gone" because nothing is obscuring my view. This is what I want for you, my fellow woman of faith. I want you to boldly remove the patriarchal, male-centered, purity-culture lenses that obscure your vision when you read scripture. I don't believe the women in scripture are merely supporting characters, presented only to model docility and submissiveness to keep you in line. No, our sisters in the Bible have much more to say, and I believe what's on these pages will give our women of scripture a fresh voice.

This book is not just a traditional Bible study guide. It's a reclamation—a chance for you to reclaim all the parts of yourself—the spirituality, sensuality, self-worth, and yes, even sexiness—that have been held captive by male-centered teachings. Your faith and femininity don't have to fight each other. You don't have to choose between your holiness and your wholeness. God wants you to experience both.

This book also draws from the Bible studies I've led in The House of Women—studies that have consistently liberated so many women to embrace their faith, femininity, and sexiness. In these Bible studies, we use my Signature S5 Lifestyle to help us embrace what's necessary to be fully set free as women of faith. This includes embracing our spirituality, sensuality, sexuality, self-worth, and supportive sisterhood. The women in Scripture have proven to illuminate this framework in a way that liberates and strengthens us.

Like many other women of faith, I was taught to view the women in Scripture as problems to be solved, hindrances to the purpose of our brothers, or background supporters to men. They were seen as footnotes to the story rather than complex, influential individuals with their own stories. I've sat in Bible studies and sermons that left me drowning in shame, fear, and judgment. But thanks be to God, this is not what God wants for us when we read the Scriptures.

This book was written because you deserve to see yourself in Scripture—not through patriarchal or purity-culture conditioned sunglasses—but as a woman who can liberate and empower yourself to be happy, healed, and whole.

I know there will be objections and critiques of this book. Some will call it too progressive, anti-traditional, or even anti-men. But freedom doesn't only free women; it frees everybody! When we remove the harmful ideologies and hurtful expressions of faith that cause so much pain, those around us can experience God in a holistic, healing, thriving, and liberating way. One of the most significant objections to experiencing this freedom is the fear of false teachings and being led astray. Fear often holds us captive, even from the goodness of the gospel - one of God's best gifts.

Imagine avoiding apples because you fear choking alone. That was me. I developed this irrational fear that if I didn't chew my luscious apple slices several times, I would choke on my own and meet a horrible, single woman's demise because of... apples. But that's how many of us approach our faith: terrified of choking on "false teachings" and dying a spiritual death. This fear-focused mindset causes us to miss out on God's beauty for us. Let this book, along with the Holy Spirit, be your GPS, guiding you on a journey free of fear, rooted in liberation and truth.

"FREEDOM DOESN'T ONLY FREE WOMEN; IT FREES EVERYBODY!"

WHO THIS BOOK IS FOR

You have this book in your hands because you're exhausted by theologies and teachings that deny the fullness of your womanhood. For some, it may feel like you're in a cage. You feel like your religion, your church, your upbringing, and your theology have contained you, and you want to be set free. You're not looking for excuses to do wrong. You're not looking for excuses to stray. You're not looking for excuses to live in sin. You're not looking for a reason to avoid discipline or growth pains. But you ARE looking for a faith that frees up the best parts of you, invites your whole self to the table, and allows you to embrace your freedom in Christ wholeheartedly. You are looking for a relationship with God that supports the beauty you have, the body you have, and even the sexiness you have. You want a relationship with God that opens you up to new possibilities you haven't yet experienced.

I pray that the pages of this book will provide guidance, clarity, and a fresh perspective to studying women in scripture through a womanist lens so that it unshackles you from old ways of thinking and nudges you toward something new. As you turn the pages, approach these women in Scripture like your girlfriends—with wisdom, insight, and stories that resonate. What would Eve say if she knew you wanted to live fully, boldly, and free of shame? What wisdom would Hagar share about resilience and reclaiming your worth? These women's lives hold secrets, wisdom, and love—if we only listen. Sensitive topics are ahead, so go at your own pace. I've included reflection questions to deepen your understanding and help you process what you're learning in your own context.

Ultimately, I believe the Bible can liberate us in all areas of our lives. So, as you study, I invite you to spend time with your Creator, soak in the gems found in God's word and allow the Spirit of God to speak to you as you go on this journey.

Let's spend time together through the pages of this book because it's time for us to be set free—to see ourselves as God intended: flawed but fierce, sensual but saintly, holy and unapologetic in our womanhood and faith. You're not just receiving theology; I'm inviting you to live fully in God's truth. You're here because you know you're ready—ready to be free, ready to dance, ready to see God in ways that invite your whole self into His story. You're here because your faith and femininity don't have to be at odds. God's heart for you is freedom in every part of who you are.

LET'S SET THE STAGE

Before we delight in the gems that shine brightly through the lives of these ancient women, let's take a moment to imagine the world they inhabited. What follows is a brief overview—a snapshot to help set the stage for our journey. This is not an exhaustive exploration of history or culture, nor is it meant to be a textbook. Instead, consider it an invitation, a starting point to whet your appetite for further discovery. I encourage you to seek out additional resources to delve deeper into the rich history and complex societal structures that shaped their lives.

If we were in a museum observing a portrait of their world, we would see a community painted by a pervasive system called patriarchy, where men held authority, property, and power. It defined the social, political, and economic structures of the ancient Near East. It often confined women to secondary roles, where their worth was measured by how many sons they could bear or how well they kept a home. And yet, these were women who lived, worked, and found ways to survive—even thrive. Even with these restrictions that colored their existence, women's lives were beautifully complex, vibrant, and full of quiet resilience. I invite you to become a curious explorer, stepping into a land where being a woman was a valuable but complicated journey overflowing with lessons and gems for us to discover today.

Take marriage, for instance. Love? Often optional. No mushy R&B songs here. Marriage was a strategic alliance between families to consolidate wealth and ensure lineage. Imagine being a young girl with no say in whom she would marry, her life decided by the men around her. This was the norm. Divorce, if it happened, was usually up to the man, not the woman. Remarriage? Also heavily stigmatized. And yet, we'll find stories of women who carved out power and purpose even within these strict boundaries.

Economically, women were largely dependent on men. They relied on men to own property, inherit wealth, and control financial resources, almost always exclusively in men's hands. Yes, there are instances in Scripture where we see Lydia, the merchant of purple, or Tamar, who took bold actions to secure her future, but these are typically the exceptions, not the rule. Most women relied on either their male relatives or their husbands for support. Beyond economic dependency, think about our sisters' daily, unseen labor. They cultivated crops, prepared food, and cared for livestock—often remaining largely invisible. Their work was taken for granted and seldom valued as much as what the men were doing.

Building on that foundation, the social realm of women was similarly confined to several strict gender roles and expectations. They often lived within a domestic sphere, responsible for childcare and meal preparation. Education was not always accessible to women, limiting their intellectual and social advancement opportunities. Of course, there are always exceptions—women with exceptionally high social status and some level of freedom and influence. However, most women during this time were subject to the men in their lives. Even adultery, for example, was a grave offense for women, often carrying enormous, horrifying consequences, whereas men were granted latitude.

In religious life, women often found themselves excluded from rituals and roles, sidelined by customs and laws that reinforced patriarchy. Thankfully, we have a beautiful sprinkling of women who took up spiritual responsibilities, like Miriam the Levite, Deborah the Judge, and Queen Esther. We have prophets, judges, and queens whose voices rose above societal limits. God intervened in their lives, breaking through the barriers set up by culture to accomplish work through them.

THE GEOGRAPHICAL STAGE

Let's also briefly focus on where these women lived—the lands that shaped their daily reality. There was the Fertile Crescent, the cradle of civilization, home to various cultures and societies. The land was lush and productive, encompassing what we would now consider modern-day Iraq, Syria, Lebanon, Jordan, Egypt, and Israel. Many of these modern-day locations will serve as the setting for many of the biblical narratives we will explore in this book. This region had varied geography. The mountains of Lebanon and the rich plains of Mesopotamia—each of these geographical features influenced the people's lives and work, especially the women who labored to survive.

CANAAN

Then there is Canaan, the biblical name for what we would consider modern-day Israel, Palestine, and parts of Jordan. Canaan was like a mosaic, filled with the Jebusites, the Hivites, the Perizzites, the Hittites, the Amorites, and the Canaanites. These different nations brought their unique cultural practices, social structures, religions, and belief systems. If a Canaanite woman lived there, her life would have been complex, with varied expectations depending on her community. Although arranged marriages and fertility were prized, some high-status women, like Queen Jezebel, found a measure of independence within the constraints of patriarchy.

THE ISRAELITES

The Israelites were nomads, bringing a distinct monotheistic faith and worldview. Their lives centered on a covenantal way of living, including women. The Law of Moses was essential, and it provided particular guidelines—especially for women—that ensured their dignity, health, and protection. Still, patriarchal structures had a significant impact on the lives of Israelite women. Marriage was essential. Childbearing was of extreme importance. And Israelite women largely held domestic roles. There were always exceptions, like Deborah and other women, but generally, women during the Israelite period were devoted to the home.

JUDEA AND SAMARIA

Moving to Judea and Samaria, we encounter a divided legacy. When the kingdom split, the Israelite kingdom was divided between Judah and Israel, which was a significant turning point. Judea was centered around Jerusalem and the temple, and they followed the traditions of Israelite laws and customs. At the same time, Samaria had a more diverse population and was exposed to more foreign influences, resulting in a much more socially diverse landscape. Imagine how a woman's life would differ if she were raised in Judea's strict traditions versus Samaria's melting pot.

PERSIAN AND GREEK INFLUENCE

The Persian rule brought some level of stability and minor advancements for women. For example, Persian law granted women specific property and inheritance rights. We see this in the courageous story of Queen Esther and Queen Vashti. Still, patriarchal residue remained no matter where you went. While they had influence and levels of authority, the king could overrule them by either banishing them or threatening Esther with death if she approached him at the wrong time. Later, the Hellenistic period brought a Greek influence. This era opened doors for women, as Greek culture offered opportunities for education, independence, and participation in public settings. While these changes were happening more in cities and urban areas, they rippled into women's lives in Judea.

ROME AND NAZARETH

Nazareth is where Jesus was raised. It was considered a small town in Galilee, providing a glimpse into what women's lives would have looked like in Biblical times. Although Nazareth is often minimized or overshadowed by events in other towns in Judea and Samaria, it's still provides a snapshot of what was happening in larger areas. Women in Galilee experienced the same level of patriarchy and patriarchal issues while leveraging the opportunities available. Ultimately, Nazareth is still worth mentioning because Jesus was there.

Women would have had a front-row seat to the radical demolition of gender and societal norms Jesus encountered while living in Nazareth. What a gift!

Roman rule brought significant changes, as Roman law granted women more rights than previous systems. Women could own property, though not equally with men. Urbanization created opportunities for women in trade and service industries, but patriarchal structures remained dominant, particularly in the family. When the temple in Jerusalem was destroyed, losing that central place of worship, Jewish women faced new challenges and changes as traditions and structures were disrupted.

AND YET... NOT MUCH HAS CHANGED

And here we are, looking back at these ancient lives, yet realizing how much hasn't changed. Women today still face versions of these struggles. In many parts of the world, the legacy of patriarchy and male dominance is as alive as ever. We've made strides, yes, but in countless communities, countries, and cultures, women's voices are stifled, their worth measured by their domestic roles or their ability to bear children. In some places, property rights, education, and even safety remain privileges rather than rights for women. The same resilient spirit that empowered our sisters then remains necessary now, whether in a remote village where girls are denied schooling or in systems that continue to limit women's potential.

THESE STORIES MATTER TODAY

So, this is the world of our sisters in Scripture—a world often defined by patriarchy and male dominance. While patriarchy provided a structured system that shaped ancient societies—offering order, lineage preservation, and male-centered stability—it did so at the expense of women's autonomy, agency, and well-being. Some may argue that it was "necessary for the time," but let's be honest: what was necessary for men often came at the cost of women's freedom. This book is not here to rehabilitate patriarchy, dress it up, and make it palatable. I am not here to put lipstick and a bow on oppression and call it "balance". I am here to tell the truth. And the truth is, patriarchy was a problem for women in scripture, and it remains a problem today. My mission is to call it out—not to romanticize it—so that we, as women of faith, can step into the fullness of who God has called us to be: liberated, whole, and unashamed.

These women were not passive bystanders. They were mothers, sisters, leaders, daughters, wives, and survivors. Their stories may be hidden behind the viewpoint of men, but when we dig deeper, we'll uncover stories of resilience, courage, and strength. These women made a way out of no way, and through their lives, we're about to learn some of the most profound lessons about life, love, and relationships.

1

LESSONS
FROM EVE

Location: Garden of Eden, outside of Eden
(Genesis 2:8; Genesis 3:23)

RELATIONSHIP STATUS: MARRIED

FAST FACTS:

♦ Her name means "mother of all living." (Genesis 3:20)

♦ She was created from Adam's rib. (Genesis 2:21-22)

♦ She ate the fruit first, but she represents the genesis of God's redemptive plan for humankind. (Genesis 3:6; Romans 5:12-15)

LIFE EVENTS

♦ Created by God to be Adam's helper and companion/partner (Genesis 2:18)

♦ Talked to a serpent (Genesis 3:1-5)

♦ Gave birth to Cain, Abel, and Seth, and they continued the lineage that eventually led to the birth of Jesus (Genesis 4:1-2, 25; Luke 3:38)

♦ Experienced the grief of losing a son and the tragedy of a son murdering his brother (Genesis 4:8, 25)

THE WOMEN WHO CAN RELATE

♦ Women who have made life-changing mistakes with lifelong consequences

♦ Women who are often unfairly blamed for things and long to just be seen as human instead of a problem

♦ Mothers who have experienced profound loss from losing a child or loved one

♦ Women who are strongly connected to their spouse

♦ Women who are trailblazers, who are the first in their families or communities to do something of significance that carry a heavy weight for generations

♦ Women who wrestle with temptation

Eve's story isn't just the tale of humanity's first woman—it reflects many of our struggles. She was created to partner with Adam, yet her life goes far beyond the Garden, touching on universal themes of connection, temptation, loss, and redemption. As the "mother of all living," Eve is the origin of God's redemptive plan, symbolizing vulnerability and strength. Her story resonates with women who carry the weight of expectation, have made choices with lasting consequences, and are often misunderstood. Eve reminds us that mistakes don't define us; they bring color to our existence. As we explore her life, let's uncover the timeless lessons she offers for our own.

1

WE WERE MADE FOR CONNECTION

> *"The Lord God said, 'It is not good for the man to be alone. I will make a helper suitable for him.'" (Genesis 2:18)*

Yes, Eve was made in the image of God and the likeness of God. She was also created to be connected and in a relationship with Adam. Her existence was made for Adam. Her existence was for the express purpose of connecting with someone. It cannot be overlooked that her presence came with a partner ready to connect and choose her.

Does this mean we were created only to be with a man? Not at all. But it's okay to acknowledge that we're wired for connection and relationships that mirror God's deep love for us. God, Elohim, is a relational God, existing as Father, Son, and Holy Spirit—a community of love. For God to be God, He had to be in communion with others.

In the same way, being made in His image means we, too, are designed for connection. It's how we're built. We're wired for intimacy, relationships, and meaningful bonds that fulfill our soul's need to be known and to know others. When Genesis 2:18 says, "It is not good for the man to be alone," this verse isn't just about Adam; it's a universal truth. We, as social creatures, crave connection. It's wired into our DNA. Think about times in your own life when you felt most alive and fulfilled.

Wasn't it when loved ones surrounded you, sharing laughter, offering support, and simply being present with each other?

I used to have a favorite watch that I wore everywhere. But one day, a link in the chain broke and went missing, leaving it unwearable. The entire watch became useless without that one link—the piece that held it all together. Just like the chain on my watch was broken and in need of repair and couldn't be used, you have permission to admit that you need repair if you lack deep, meaningful, intimate connections with others. It doesn't always have to be a romantic partner, but you were wired for a relationship, and there's absolutely nothing wrong with living into that need and acknowledging it. It could be with family, friends, or your community. But we were designed for relationships. Acknowledging this need isn't weakness— it's living into how God created us.

This realization is also why casual "situationships" never worked for me. At first, they scratched an itch. The men I was with served as placeholders, and it was a good time—a great time. But brewing beneath the surface was the realization that this wasn't a real connection. We connected to some degree, but it wasn't a relationship. It was fabricated in fantasy, not reality. It lacked depth and reciprocity because there wasn't a commitment to remain connected. Together, but not really together. This is not what God wants for us.

There's a time for casual connections, yes. But it's different when looking for sincere, meaningful, and lasting intimacy. Genuine connection calls us into something deeper, something natural and intentional. And ultimately, that's what we were created for. Eve reminds us that we were created for a real connection, not a superficial one.

The Gem Being Dropped:

Don't ever apologize for your need and desire for connection. It's a part of who you are. Embrace, honor, and let it guide you to seek connections that nourish your soul.

2

OUR SEXUALITY IS PART OF GOD'S IMAGE

"So God created mankind in his own image, in the image of God he created them; male and female he created them." (Genesis 1:27)

"Adam and his wife were both naked, and they felt no shame." (Genesis 2:25)

Eve also reminds us that who we are as women isn't dirty or something to be ashamed of. It's not only how we were created, but it is a reflection of the image of God. When we look in the mirror, we see wrinkles, lumps, stretch marks, and curves, forgetting that this body we inhabit—this sexual body—is also a reflection of who God is: a creator, a lover, and an advocate for pleasure to be experienced deeply within ourselves.

Your sexuality is a wonderful, wholesome part of who you are. Eve reminds us of this. We often emphasize the maleness of God, but Eve reminds us that our sexuality is not only in the mind of God, but it's a reflection of who God is—a God that produces, a God that creates, a God that brings things into being. A God that loves.

Our sexuality being a reflection of God's image also means that it's complicated and multi-faceted. One woman's expression of sexuality won't be the same as another's. But in the creative mind of God, that makes sense because God never intended for our sexuality to look robotically the same. Just take in nature around us, and you will quickly see that God never intended us to be the same. Some elements never change, but their expression will be diverse and creative. Our sexuality and how it is expressed is a reflection of the diversity of human beings. God is understood as a unity of three persons in diversity. The diversity of human sexuality, including female sexuality, may reflect the diversity within God's image.

Now, before you get your traditional, conservative beliefs all hot and bothered, I'm speaking about how our sexuality is expressed. Some women feel sexy by wearing heels. Others prefer flats. Some women feel aroused with nipple play, while others would prefer you lean into their neck and go to town. One isn't better than the other— it's simply diverse expressions of our sexuality. The resistance that comes to the surface when we speak of our sexuality in this context is rooted in control and oppression and must be confronted and rooted out. How we express and live in our sexual bodies will be different, and that's okay.

I think about going to buffet restaurants, and for that restaurant to remain in business, they have to provide an array of options.

There has to be variety. Nobody would come if they had the same type of chicken but still called itself a buffet. The same thing applies to our human sexuality. There will be variances in expression. If anything, Christian women would do well to broaden the scope of what it means to express oneself sexually so that our spaces are more inclusive. We probably wouldn't have as many outsiders and marginalized groups of women if we erased the lines that leave those who are different out. Another reason why Eve teaches us that our sexuality is part of God's image is that when we realize our sexuality is part of God's image, it also means that it's good.

Very good. It's not a problem, not an issue, not a sin, not something to be ashamed of, but it's good. Very good. Good things are to be treasured. Good things are to be celebrated and enjoyed. Good things are to be indulged in and expressed. And that's just a good thing. Imagine how many more VERY good things you can experience. Remember, God creates good things, and that includes our sexuality.

When we acknowledge that our sexuality is part of God's image, we're also saying that our feelings of desire and arousal are holy and sacred. They reflect a God who is also a God of love. Eve is reminding us that our deep desire for emotional connection through sex can be seen as reflecting the relational nature of God. When those feelings bubble to the surface, they are a reminder of who God is and who God created us to be. I think of kettles and boiling water. It's not a problem for the water to get hot. It's not an issue for it to boil. What matters is how we use the hot water. Likewise, our hot, burning, horny desires are meant to fill us up and overwhelm us. What's key is how we manage and direct those desires in ways that honor God, our bodies, and each other.

"ONE WOMAN'S EXPRESSION OF SEXUALITY WON'T BE THE SAME AS ANOTHER'S!"

The Gem Being Dropped:

Eve was created with a unique feminine sexuality, and guess what—it was perfect. Your sexuality isn't something to fear or hide; it's a beautiful part of who you are.

3

THE RIGHT MAN WILL LOVE MORE THAN YOUR BODY

> *"This is now bone of my bones and flesh of my flesh; she shall be called 'woman,' for she was taken out of man."*
> *(Genesis 2:23)*

Growing up, I would hear preachers bark out that Adam marveled at Eve's hips, lips, and fingertips. They would go on and on about her Coca-Cola body shape and gorgeous appearance. I suppose this was their sanctified imagination, but understand this is nowhere in the text, and it's a somewhat lazy approach to explaining what was happening. I want to apologize on behalf of all preachers who make women who don't have a 'Coca-Cola body' feel some type of way. There are plenty of shenanigans happening in pulpits to objectify the bodies of women to get some "amens" and cackles from the pews.

What was happening was that Adam laid eyes on Eve for the first time, declaring this was "bone of my bone and flesh of my flesh." He was actually declaring that this woman was of the same substance. She's of the same self as me. I can love who she is because I see myself in her and can be connected to her. She's unlike any of the animals

I've encountered, but she is...me. She has hair like me, eyes like me, fingers like me. This can work because we're of the same kind. We're using the same model and manufacturer.

When you go to the car dealership for a specific brand, the cars don't look all the same, but there are specific and unique things that every car for that brand has. For example, my Lexus has that unique clock, just like every other manufactured Lexus. Likewise, Adam was saying, she's a Lexus like me! I love who she is because I can relate to her. We understand each other. We can be close to each other. Our bodies fit together. There's an intimacy, a connection that can be created that I can't manufacture anywhere else. I love the dog, but the dog isn't me. I love lions, bears, and birds, but they're not me. But Eve. She's me. I'm her.

Eve also experienced Adam's appreciation and delight in having someone he could value and understand. He was enjoying the uniqueness of her beauty and glory because although they were the same, there were slight differences that excited him. He saw her as someone worth cherishing and enjoying because my bones and flesh are valuable too.

Hear me, ladies. Your partner will marvel at and cherish you when he recognizes that loving himself makes room to love you, too. A man will cherish and value you when he sees beyond the physical and realizes you're a woman he can deeply connect with and relate to. It'll almost be like an exhale, finally someone like me. We came from the same place, so I had to care for her. I valued and treated her like I would treat myself because we were the same. A man can only do that when he recognizes who he is so he can love who you are.

So trust me, whether you're a size 2 or 24 or somewhere in between, the right man will love how you show up in the world because he will see your worth, he'll see himself in you, and he'll be able to connect and relate to you. Your worth is not defined by whether you look like Eve or not. It's not rooted in what society currently deems as attractive. It's rooted in your identity as a woman created in the image of God. And you're worthy of a man declaring, this is bone of my bone and flesh of my flesh, just like Eve was.

The Gem Being Dropped:

When Adam first laid eyes on Eve, he didn't just say, "She's alright." No, he waxed poetic: "This is now bone of my bones and flesh of my flesh" (Genesis 2:23). The right man will cherish you, just as you are.

4

PATRIARCHY IS A CONSEQUENCE OF SIN, NOT THE ORIGINAL DESIGN

"So God created mankind in his own image... male and female he created them." (Genesis 1:27)

"Your desire will be for your husband, and he will rule over you." (Genesis 3:16)

I was on a date with a gentleman, and it went well until we veered into a conversation about his views on gender roles. He believed that men have specific roles that are different from women's because men are more intelligent and stronger. He sincerely believed that God designed men to have stronger brains than women from creation. Needless to say, there was not a second date. As wild as this belief is, variances of this ideology persist in society. How we interpret the Eve story has been influential in shaping social attitudes toward gender roles and the justification of oppressive patriarchal structures that are downright ludicrous. Women have been told that because Adam was created first and Eve was made from Adam's rib, it means that men have power and importance over women. Women have been told that since Eve was created as a helper for Adam, we are seen as primary assistants and helpers for men.

I don't have time in this book to debunk these myths, but I want to focus on a specific one regarding subordination and headship. Some people believe that because God told Adam that he would rule over Eve, it means we are subject to being bossed around and controlled by men as punishment. This scripture has been misused to support the submission and control of women by suggesting that this was the setup from the beginning. However, this view is inconsistent with the liberating, freeing power of the gospel of Jesus Christ. It is reckless and irresponsible to teach that when God made it official that Eve would be ruled by her husband, this was intended to be beneficial and necessary for women to be women and succeed. Don't you dare believe for a second that your worth is less because you're a woman! Or that it would help if you were automatically ruled over and controlled because of who you are. Eve's subordination was a consequence of sin (Genesis 3:16), not God's blueprint for creation. We were all created equally in His image. Eve's story challenges the harmful belief that women are inherently inferior to men. Genesis 1:27 tells us that both men and women were created "in the image of God." This establishes our inherent equality and value before God. The concept of male dominance arose from the fall, not God's original plan. If God wanted Adam to rule over Eve as part of the blueprint, it would've been mentioned before Genesis 3 when God was giving instructions on ruling over animals and being fruitful and multiplying. There are clear instructions to rule over creation, not over each other.

Further, the words were given to Eve, not Adam. "And he shall rule over you" — not "Adam, you shall rule over her." This text is not a command for husbands to rule over their wives. Instead, it was the pronouncement of rebuke to Eve after introducing sin into the world. Seeking out a gender hierarchy was never presented as something good or a posture to seek after. Just like women don't look forward to childbearing pains, according to this text, women shouldn't be looking for or purposely placing themselves in situations to be ruled over. Because who intentionally seeks to punish themselves? That's why we have anesthesia and do all we can to lessen the pain of childbirth. Don't allow a distorted interpretation of Eve's story to hold you back. Don't allow social expectations to make you okay with a man who demands to be your boss. Avoid relationships that prioritize punishing you with rulership instead of loving you with equal partnership. You are capable, intelligent, and created with unique gifts to share with the world. And you deserve a relationship where you are an equal partner.

"AVOID RELATIONSHIPS THAT PRIORITIZE PUNISHING YOU WITH RULERSHIP INSTEAD OF LOVING YOU WITH EQUAL PARTNERSHIP!"

The Gem Being Dropped:

Reject any limitations placed on you because of your gender. Embrace your God-given strengths and pursue your dreams with confidence. Remember, Eve wasn't created to be a follower; she was designed to be a partner, walking alongside Adam.

5

SEXUALITY CAN BE REDEEMED FROM THE CONSEQUENCES OF SIN

"Then the eyes of both of them were opened, and they realized they were naked, so they sewed fig leaves together and made coverings for themselves." (Genesis 3:7)

"Christ redeemed us from the curse of the law by becoming a curse for us..." (Galatians 3:13)

Sexuality got a bit skewed after that whole fruit incident. But thank God for Jesus! He took the curse for us, restoring everything, including our sexuality, back to its intended glory. The story of Eve and the Forbidden Fruit can sometimes lead to the misconception that our sexuality is inherently linked to shame and sin. However, a deeper look reveals the possibility of redemption and a return to God's original design for our sexual expression.

Ancient cultures often viewed women's sexuality with suspicion and fear. Women were either revered or reviled, with little space for a holistic understanding of their humanity. This perspective seeped into some interpretations of the Bible, fueling narratives that connected female sexuality to temptation and sin. However, it's crucial to remember that the Garden of Eden existed before sin entered the world. In its untouched state, Adam and Eve's nakedness wasn't a source of shame but a testament to their purity, vulnerability, and intimacy with God. There's no reason to believe sexuality itself was sinful in that context—it was part of God's original creation, intended to reflect His glory.

The good news is that Jesus' sacrifice on the cross covers all of sin's consequences, including the distortion of our sexuality. Through a relationship with Him, we can experience healing, shed shame, and rediscover the beauty and purpose of God's gift of sexuality.

Think of sexuality like a river. When flowing in its intended path, a river provides life, sustenance, and beauty. But when blocked or diverted, it can cause destruction or stagnation. Sin diverted the river of sexuality, distorting its flow and purpose. But Jesus acts as the master engineer, removing blockages and redirecting its course back to life-giving waters. This redemption doesn't erase the challenges that come with living in a broken world, but it offers hope for a journey toward wholeness.

Consider how African American spirituals reclaimed pain and oppression and transformed them into powerful expressions of hope and faith. In a similar way, Jesus takes the parts of our stories marred by sin and shame—including our sexual stories—and reclaims them, transforming them into testimonies of healing, grace, and restoration.

The redemption Jesus offers isn't just about avoiding sin; it's about flourishing within God's original design. His sacrifice allows us to see our sexuality not as a curse or a source of shame but as a sacred gift. When we embrace God's redemptive power, we aren't just healed; we're restored to the wholeness He intended from the start.

The Gem Being Dropped:

Your sexuality is not a curse; it's a gift wrapped in God's grace. Jesus didn't just redeem your soul—He redeemed your story, including the parts stained by shame. When you embrace God's redemptive power, you're not just healed—you're restored to the wholeness God designed from the start. Your sexuality isn't something to fear or hide; it's a sacred reflection of His creativity, meant to be celebrated within His divine plan. Because of Jesus, you can experience a more fulfilling and Christ-centered expression of your sexuality.

TIME TO DROP YOUR OWN GEMS:

- How can you cultivate deeper connections in your life, reflecting God's design for us?
- What steps can you take to embrace your sexuality as a good and beautiful part of you?
- How can you learn to fully appreciate and love your body for yourself, regardless of relationship status, letting your self-worth come from within rather than how others see you?
- How can you embrace the beauty of being seen and cherished by a partner while staying rooted in a love for your body independent of any gaze?
- How can you live in the redemption Jesus offers for your sexuality and every aspect of your life?

2

LESSONS FROM SARAH

Location: Canaan, Ur of the Chaldees (Genesis 11:31; Genesis 12:5)

RELATIONSHIP STATUS: MARRIED

FAST FACTS

◆ God changed her name to Sarah from Sarai (Genesis 17:15)

◆ She became a mother at the young age of 90 years old (Genesis 17:17; Genesis 21:1-2)

◆ She's known for her belly laugh (Genesis 18:12-15)

◆ She's mentioned in the NT as a woman of faith (Hebrews 11:11; 1 Peter 3:6)

LIFE EVENTS

- Left home to follow her man to a place she didn't know she was going (Genesis 12:1-5)
- Pretended to be Abraham's sister twice (Genesis 12:11-13; Genesis 20:2)
- Struggled with infertility (Genesis 16:1-2)
- She had beef with her servant Hagar (Genesis 16:4-6; Genesis 21:9-10)
- She gave birth to her son Isaac at an older age (Genesis 21:1-3)

THE WOMEN WHO CAN RELATE

- Women who struggle with infertility or struggle with having children later in life
- Women who feel their beauty is a threat or a problem
- Women who had to deal with relationships with "the other woman."
- Women who have mean-girl tendencies
- Women experiencing tension in their marriage or relationships
- Women who laugh in joy or shock when God says God will do something outrageous in your life

Have you found yourself crying one moment and then laughing the next? Sarah could relate. Her life proves that a woman's journey is filled with complicated and layered emotions. She shows us that you've truly tapped into the human experience when your life is filled with rollercoasters of love, ugly feelings, deep belly laughs, and bold promises fulfilled. She followed her husband Abraham into the unknown, endured societal pressures, and bore a son at 90, showcasing resilience and vulnerability. Her story reminds us of the beauty, complexity, and strength that define a woman's journey.

1

DON'T UNDERESTIMATE WHAT YOUR BODY CAN DO AT ANY AGE

"Is anything too hard for the LORD? At the appointed time, I will return to you, according to the time of life, and Sarah shall have a son." (Genesis 18:14)

"By faith Sarah herself also received strength to conceive seed, and she bore a child when she was past the age, because she judged Him faithful who had promised." (Hebrews 11:11)

As of December 2023, Safina Namukwaya, a 70-year-old Ugandan woman, is considered one of the oldest women to give birth. Namukwaya gave birth to twins, a boy and a girl, via C-section at a fertility clinic in Kampala using donor eggs and her partner's sperm. She also gave birth to a daughter at the same facility in 2020 in her late 60s. Namukwaya told local media that giving birth was a "miracle."

Like Safina, who experienced the miracle and mystery of giving birth at her age, Sarah's story is not a fairytale but a powerful testament to the belief that age is a whisper against the roar of what our bodies can achieve at any age. Despite being well beyond the typical age for childbearing, Sarah conceived and bore Isaac, fulfilling a promise made by God. This miracle, detailed in Genesis 18:9-15 and Hebrews 11:11, underscores our physical and sexual capabilities are not strictly bound by age. It invites us to reconsider and celebrate our bodies' potential at every stage of life, challenging societal norms that often devalue older women's physical and sexual vitality.

Years ago, my dad planted a tree in our backyard. At first, it was just a sapling needing support to remain upright. But as the years went on, it grew stronger and taller. It's been a joy to witness the growth of this tree. As the tree gets older, its branches may not be as flexible, but its roots run deep, offering strength for us to climb and resilience young trees haven't yet developed. Just like our tree grew stronger and wiser, our bodies may change with age, but they gain experience, wisdom, and a different kind of strength as we mature. Like a mighty oak, our bodies may lose youthful suppleness, but their roots dig deep, gaining resilience and wisdom each year.

In Sarah's time, fertility was a significant aspect of a woman's value in society, and barrenness was often seen as a curse. Thus, Sarah's late-in-life pregnancy defied not only biological expectations but also societal norms, highlighting a divine intervention that redefines what is considered possible.

Sarah's story shatters the myth that a woman's potential diminishes with age. According to human limitations, God's promise seemed impossible, yet Sarah eventually conceived and gave birth to Isaac, a miracle that defied expectations. This reminds us, sisters, that God's timing is perfect and our bodies are capable of amazing things at any stage of life.

"OUR BODIES ARE CAPABLE OF AMAZING THINGS AT ANY STAGE OF LIFE."

The Gem Being Dropped:

Don't write yourself off based on age or limitations. Our bodies are God-breathed vessels, and God can work through them unexpectedly. Embrace your body's unique journey, celebrate its strengths, and honor its wisdom.

2

YOU'RE WORTHY OF
PLEASURE AT ANY AGE

"And Sarah said, 'God has made me laugh, and all who hear will laugh with me.' She also said, 'Who would have said to Abraham that Sarah would nurse children? For I have borne him a son in his old age.'" (Genesis 21:6-7)

"You will show me the path of life; in Your presence is fullness of joy; at Your right hand are pleasures forevermore." (Psalm 16:11)

"And also that every man should eat and drink and enjoy the good of all his labor—it is the gift of God."

(Ecclesiastes 3:13)

I was a kindergarten music teacher for many years and adored my class. Their energy, unapologetic joy, and pleasure, their undignified, unrefined dancing and enjoyment of the music, watered my adult soul.

Their hearts and minds had not yet been sullied by the expectations and pressures of this world to contain their pleasure, excitement, and joy. They had not yet been introduced to the pleasure police, who insist that pleasure must be legislated and controlled based on age and gender.

So, when I read about Sarah, I think about my kindergartners. I think about whether Sarah would've laughed incredulously at the mere thought of her having a good time with her husband in the bedroom at her age if she embraced the idea that she's STILL worthy of pleasure and making pleasure-induced babies at her age. Because let's be completely real.

An excellent sexual encounter is usually a pleasurable one. Even at 90, with a little help like lubrication, her body is still capable of responding to stimulation, right?

And so, Sarah's experience speaks to the importance of recognizing one's worthiness of pleasure, regardless of age. Her joy at conceiving Isaac exemplifies the broader principle that pleasure, sexual and otherwise, is not limited to the young. In a society where aging and sexuality often seem at odds, Sarah's story is a divine affirmation that pleasure is a lifelong gift from God, meant to be embraced and enjoyed. And that includes our sexual encounters. Pleasure is not just for teenagers and the middle-aged. It's a beautiful gift from God and meant to be enjoyed throughout our lives, not just relegated to youthful fantasies. Now, Sarah's story doesn't explicitly talk about her physical intimacy with Abraham.

However, within the cultural context, we can glean some powerful truths. Remember that whole "barrenness is a curse" thing? Well, in that society, a woman's sexuality was often seen as a tool for procreation, not pleasure. But God created sex to be pleasurable for both partners, a way to express love and deepen intimacy. Think about it. Even though Sarah was beyond childbearing years, God still chose to bless her with the ability to conceive. This act, defying natural limitations, hints at the importance of intimacy and pleasure as part of God's design, even at an "advanced" age.

The Gem Being Dropped:

Our sexuality is a gift from God to be embraced and celebrated at any stage of life. Pleasure is not a selfish act; it's a way to connect with your partner and beautifully experience God's goodness.

3

JEALOUSY IS NATURAL, ESPECIALLY WHEN YOU'RE SEXUALLY CONNECTED

"So he went in to Hagar, and she conceived. And when she saw that she had conceived, her mistress became despised in her eyes. Then Sarai said to Abram, 'My wrong be upon you! I gave my maid into your embrace; and when she saw that she had conceived, I became despised in her eyes. The LORD judge between you and me.'" (Genesis 16:4-5)

"Wrath is cruel and anger a torrent, but who is able to stand before jealousy?" (Proverbs 27:4)

The text says that when Abraham slept with Hagar and got her pregnant, Sarah despised her. This word carries feelings of contempt, disdain, and looking down on somebody. Sarah's jealousy and frustration are clearly evident in how she treats Hagar. Eventually, she has Hagar banished from their estate. Her reaction speaks to a deep-seated fear of being replaced or overshadowed. Sarah's jealousy didn't emerge in a vacuum; it was compounded by cultural pressures, her barrenness, and the intimate connection between Abraham and Hagar that she herself had sanctioned but couldn't bear to witness.

Let's be honest, sisters—jealousy can rear its ugly head in even the most secure relationships. And Sarah is no exception. When Abraham, following cultural norms of the time, takes Hagar as a concubine in hopes of securing an heir, Sarah's jealousy is palpable. It was like rain clouds hovering over their relationship, casting a shadow of doubt and insecurity on what was once the sunny and bright connection between these two lovebirds. And trust me, I do understand. I can't say an inferno of fiery insecurities wouldn't also well up within me, seeing Hagar's protruding, growing belly while mine remained smooth and flat.

Realistically, jealousy is a normal human emotion, especially when our sense of security or intimacy feels threatened. But jealousy often carries a stigma, as though it's a sign of immaturity or inadequacy. But emotions aren't inherently right or wrong—they simply are. Sarah's experience reminds us that jealousy is a natural response to feeling excluded, unseen, or unvalued in a relationship, particularly when intimacy is involved. Her story reminds us that jealousy isn't a sign of weakness; it signals that something needs attention in our relationships.

I love using air fresheners in my home. My current favorite brand is the Febreze plugins with the lavender scent. But they only last for a couple months at a time. When it's time to be replaced, a blue blinking light signals to me that I need a new air freshener. Jealousy is like that blue blinking light, alerting us to areas where we may feel insecure, overlooked, or disconnected in our relationships. When we view our jealous emotions as an opportunity for introspection rather than a reason to lash out, we can transform those feelings into a pathway for growth, clarity, and even deeper intimacy.

The Gem Being Dropped:

Jealousy isn't your enemy; it's a blinking signal that something needs addressing. When you feel its grip, take a moment to identify the underlying fear or need. Then, bring it to the table in a conversation with your partner—raw, honest, and without blame. This kind of vulnerability can strengthen your relationship and create a foundation of trust and empathy. Instead of letting jealousy define the narrative, let it deepen the bond.

4

YOU HAVE MORE IN COMMON WITH "THE SIDE CHICK" THAN YOU THINK

> *"There is neither Jew nor Greek, there is neither slave nor free, there is neither male nor female; for you are all one in Christ Jesus." (Galatians 3:28)*

> *"Then she called the name of the LORD who spoke to her, You-Are-the-God-Who-Sees; for she said, 'Have I also here seen Him who sees me?'" Genesis 16:13*

Dr. Renita Weems, in her book Just A Sister Away, reflects on Sarah and Hagar, saying, "Theirs is a story of ethnic prejudice exacerbated by economic and sexual exploitation. Theirs is a story of conflict, women betraying women, and mothers conspiring against mothers. Theirs is a story of social rivalry." She also reminds us that "Sarai forgot that in a patriarchal society, she and her female slave, Hagar, had more in common as women than that which divided them as a Hebrew mistress and Egyptian slave woman." These words resonate deeply because, centuries later, society still pits women against one another, creating divisions that overlook our shared struggles.

We see this all around us. Women often quickly label each other based on appearance, behavior, or life choices. We think women who wear short skirts and plunging necklines are worse than women who dress in Michelle Obama-style dresses all the time. We believe the fully clothed woman is better than the scantily clad woman, not realizing that both types of women are susceptible to exploitation, oppression, rape culture, and abuse of power, no matter who or what they wear.

We may assume that the woman with the degree is superior to the woman without one. Or that the woman with a husband feels validated and somehow "better" than the single woman, who may feel like her worth is less without a man by her side. In reality, we are all women navigating a world that is often still built for men, and we usually miss the chance to support and uplift each other instead of letting these divisive labels define us.

Despite the patriarchal structure, imagine the support and unity that would have emerged if Sarah and Hagar had united as allies rather than rivals. They both existed in a world that had the power to exploit them. Sarah was pressured to bear a child and resorted to using Hagar as a surrogate. Hagar was forced into a role she didn't choose and, later, cast out because she represented a failure in Sarah's life. If they had come together in solidarity, fighting the real challenges of their lives—exploitation, lack of faith, and insecurity in

God's promises—they could have reshaped their story.

Hagar's story invites Christian women to reflect on themes of jealousy, competition, and solidarity among women, urging a reevaluation of how we navigate our relationships with one another in light of societal and cultural pressures. Simply put, we can't allow our relationships with other women to be exploited by the pressures of this world. How many times have we allowed these same pressures to create distance between us and another woman, or even worse, to see another woman as a threat? We, too, are influenced by these expectations, and we, too, have the power to rewrite the narrative by supporting one another.

It's so easy to judge a woman who lives or dresses differently or to feel envious of a woman who seems to have it all together. It's even easier to look down on a woman who makes different choices, who maybe stumbles or strays in ways we might not. But what if we dropped the judgment and extended compassion instead of letting these differences drive us apart? Instead of looking for reasons to compete, when you see a sister who dresses differently and has different standards and values than you, drop the respectability and love her. When you hear of a woman who's cheating or engaging in unethical behavior, pray and have compassion before being quick to throw stones. None of us are above the struggles of life, and none of us are immune to pain, loneliness, or poor decisions. Given different circumstances, we all might find ourselves in need of grace.

The reality is we need each other. Our shared experiences as women create a bond that can be powerful if we let it. Imagine if we embraced each other as allies in a world that often still doesn't fully embrace us. Let's strive to be more supportive and less suspicious of each other.

"WE CAN'T ALLOW OUR RELATIONSHIPS WITH WOMEN TO BE EXPLOITED BY THE PRESSURES OF THIS WORLD."

The Gem Being Dropped:

Let's cultivate compassion and understanding instead of competition. Build bridges instead of walls. Uplift and celebrate each other's successes. Remember, we are all on this journey together, and by joining forces, we can rewrite the script.

5

YOUR BEAUTY IS NOT A PROBLEM, EVEN WHEN MEN THINK IT IS

"And it came to pass, when he was close to entering Egypt, that he said to Sarai, his wife, 'Indeed I know that you are a woman of beautiful countenance. Therefore, it will happen, when the Egyptians see you, that they will say, "This is his wife," and they will kill me, but they will let you live. Please say you are my sister, that it may be well with me for your sake, and that I may live because of you.'" (Genesis 12:11-13)

"I will praise You, for I am fearfully and wonderfully made; marvelous are Your works, and that my soul knows very well." (Psalm 139:14)

Picture this: You're with your man at an amusement park. The lines are super long, and it's humid. You're sweaty, and you want to get to the front of the line to ride the gigantic roller coaster you've been waiting for all summer. Suddenly, your man notices another dude eyeing you closely near the front of the line. It's as if they have a "bro code" conversation with raised eyebrows and hand gestures that only men would understand. A moment later, your man gently explains that because you're so drop-dead gorgeous and beautiful, you'll both get front-row spots in line, but you must do a couple of "favors" for the dude at the front, who also thinks you're hot stuff. Then, you can go on as many rides as you want. YAY!

Sounds absurd, right? It's an extreme illustration, but that's basically what's happening here. Sarah is so gorgeous that Abram, her husband, uses her beauty as a bargaining chip to get what he wants and needs in a new territory. He instructs her to pose as his sister, letting her beauty pave the way for him in a new land. Sarah's beauty was so striking that Abram thought it might cost him his life, and rather than trust God's protection, he saw her as a tool to negotiate his safety. This story is wild—and painfully relatable. To this day, many modern women are terrified of revealing their gorgeous curves and vivacious body features for fear that a man of God will somehow abuse and exploit how pretty we are for their selfish gain and power.

Regardless of whether Abraham thought that Sarah's beauty would get him killed, it was wrong to use her beauty in that way. As usual, there is no mention of what Sarah thought about this arrangement, and it reminds us that although Sarah's thoughts on this aren't recorded, we can now speak for ourselves when men want to misuse us simply because we're cute. Your body and beauty should never be viewed as a problem to manage but as a portrait to admire and adore. God made each of us in His image, wonderfully and intentionally, and that includes your beauty. Your body, curves, and glorious features aren't threats or temptations to be subdued. They're parts of the showstopping creation that God saw as "very good."

Sarah's story encourages us to embrace our beauty confidently, without fear of objectification or misunderstanding.

But let's be honest—many of us are conditioned to downplay our beauty, to hide it, or to make ourselves small. We learn early on that "too much" beauty might make us vulnerable to unwanted attention, judgment, or even danger. We hear whispers that our curves, skin, and confidence could invite trouble or that our presence is to blame for others' actions. But Sarah's story tells us otherwise. Even in a society that didn't ask for her thoughts or honor her autonomy, her beauty was never the problem; the problem was the fear and manipulation surrounding it.

Sarah's story challenges us to resist the narrative that blames women for how men react to them. We have the right to feel beautiful and secure without the weight of someone else's fears on our shoulders. So, let's stop apologizing for the way we look, the way we shine, and the way we express ourselves. There is nothing "extra" or "too much" about you; your presence is a gift from God, a masterpiece, not a "situation" to manage.

Her story invites us to remember that we have both beauty and power—and the autonomy to say no when someone uses us as leverage. We live in a world that often wants us to make ourselves smaller, quieter, and easier to handle. But your light, beauty, and unique essence are meant to shine. And if someone feels threatened by that, that's a challenge for them to work through, not a reason for you to dim your radiance.

"YOUR BODY AND BEAUTY SHOULD NEVER BE VIEWED AS A PROBLEM TO MANAGE BUT AS A PORTRAIT TO ADMIRE AND ADORE!"

The Gem Being Dropped:

Embrace your beauty with confidence, knowing it's a gift from God. Don't dim your light or apologize for your showstopping glory. Instead, challenge the narrative that blames women for men's actions. Advocate for a world that respects and honors your autonomy and worth as a whole person beyond your physical appearance.

TIME TO DROP YOUR OWN GEMS:

- How can Sarah's story inspire you to appreciate and celebrate your body's capabilities, regardless of age?

- How can you affirm your worthiness of pleasure and joy in your life, challenging societal norms that might suggest otherwise?

- Reflecting on Sarah and Hagar's relationship, how can you foster solidarity and understanding among women in your own life, even in the face of societal pressures or personal differences?

- How has society's perception of beauty affected your self-image, and how can you reclaim a positive and empowered understanding of your beauty?

- What lessons can you draw from Sarah's story to deepen your faith and enhance your relationships, embracing your spirituality, sexuality, sensuality, and self-worth?

3

LESSONS FROM HAGAR

Location: Hagar was an Egyptian servant in Canaan before she fled to the desert. She later returned and lived in the land of Beersheba after being cast out by Abraham (Genesis 16:1; 21:14).

RELATIONSHIP STATUS: SINGLE & SURROGATE

FAST FACTS:

- Hagar was the first person in the Bible to name God, calling Him El Roi, which means "the God who sees me" (Genesis 16:13).
- Hagar's son, Ishmael, is traditionally considered the ancestor of the Arab people, making her a significant figure in multiple religious traditions.
- She is one of the few women in the Bible to experience a direct encounter with an angel (Genesis 16:7-12).

LIFE EVENTS:

- ♦ Hagar was given to Abraham as a surrogate by Sarah, leading to the birth of Ishmael (Genesis 16:3-4).

- ♦ After becoming pregnant, Hagar and Sarah's relationship became strained, leading to Hagar fleeing into the wilderness (Genesis 16:6).

- ♦ An angel of the Lord found Hagar in the desert and promised that her son would become the father of a great nation (Genesis 16:7-12).

- ♦ After Ishmael's birth, Abraham eventually cast out Hagar and Ishmael at Sarah's insistence, but God provided for them in the wilderness (Genesis 21:14-19).

THE WOMEN WHO
CAN RELATE:

- ♦ Women who've been silenced or mistreated under the guise of cultural or religious traditions.

- ♦ Women who've felt invisible, abandoned, or overlooked—yet hold onto the truth that God sees their worth and values their existence.

- ♦ Women who've had their worth reduced to their reproductive abilities or physical roles but know they are so much more.

- ♦ Women who've been forced to suppress their desires, dreams, or individuality to meet the demands of others.

♦ Women who've found strength in fleeing toxic relationships or systems, even when it meant being judged or misunderstood.

♦ Women who've been let down by authority figures in the church or trusted spaces but are now discovering God's faithfulness in new, authentic ways.

♦ Women who've faced single motherhood, especially in difficult or unjust circumstances.

She's often seen as the footnote of the story—the side chick who got in the way of God's promises. But Hagar's story is one of an Egyptian woman's exploitation and persecution at the hands of her Hebrew mistress, Sarah. In her book, Texts of Terror, Phyllis Trible says, "All we who are heirs of Sarah and Abraham, by flesh and spirit, must answer for the terror in Hagar's story. To neglect the theological challenge she presents is to falsify faith." Despite the tragic circumstances surrounding her story, I believe Hagar can also teach us to follow the God-given desires of our hearts. Even in the face of adversity, difficulty, and struggle, her heart still wanted what it wanted, and she didn't apologize for it. The same goes for us today.

1

YOU'RE MORE THAN A BABYMAKING MACHINE

"Then Sarai, Abram's wife, took Hagar her maid, the Egyptian, and gave her to her husband Abram to be his wife, after Abram had dwelt ten years in the land of Canaan. So he went in to Hagar, and she conceived." (Genesis 16:3-4)

"But now, thus says the Lord, who created you, O Jacob, and He who formed you, O Israel: 'Fear not, for I have redeemed you; I have called you by your name; you are Mine." (Isaiah 43:1)

Hagar's story forces us to confront a truth that's as old as time itself: a woman's worth is not defined by her ability to bear children. In that ancient society, a woman's purpose was seen as intertwined with motherhood. Hagar's value was based solely on her potential to provide an heir for Abraham.

But Hagar is more than just a womb. She's a woman with hopes, dreams, and a yearning for love and security. The minute we reduce ourselves or others to mere vessels for procreation, we diminish the richness of the human experience. Delores Williams, in Sisters in the Wilderness, draws attention to how using another person's body as a surrogate for one's own is part of the slavery narrative. She explains that just as a slave's muscles were exploited for the benefit of the master, so too was a slave woman's womb. Sarai plans for Hagar's womb to be the way that Sarai herself will be built up. Abram agrees, and Hagar must comply. Williams identifies the "forced motherhood," "single motherhood," and "surrogate motherhood" Hagar experienced as themes that have long been part of Black women's lives. Inspired by Williams's insights, we can commit to doing better at supporting and advocating for women who have endured these challenges.

And yet, I find myself wrestling with the same question. Because of cardiovascular issues and complications with fibroids, I've had to seriously consider whether it's worth hanging on to my uterus if it means risking my health—or whether I should let it go and let go of the possibility of having children. These thoughts are heavy, and when I face them, I'm tempted to wonder if I'm less of a woman because I might not have children.

It's hard to unlearn the subtle ways society has ingrained this in us. Hagar's story reminds me that my value isn't determined by what my womb can or cannot do. My worth is tied to the One who calls me by name, the One who sees me for who I am—apart from what my body can produce.

The Gem Being Dropped:

Your value extends far beyond your reproductive potential. Embrace your talents, passions, and unique gifts. Don't let anyone, not even yourself, tell you that your worth is tied to having children.

2

GOD SEES YOU. ALWAYS.

"Then she called the name of the Lord who spoke to her, 'You-Are-the-God-Who-Sees;' for she said, 'Have I also here seen Him who sees me?'" (Genesis 16:13)

"The eyes of the Lord are on the righteous, and His ears are open to their cry." (Psalm 34:15)

Hagar's story takes a heartbreaking turn when Sarai, after finally conceiving, begins to mistreat her. Ostracized and desperate, Hagar flees into the wilderness with her young son, Ishmael. Lost and alone, she feels abandoned by everyone—including God.

But in her despair, an angel appears to her. This divine encounter reminds us of an unshakable truth: God sees us. Even in the darkest, most desolate corners of our lives, He doesn't turn His back. He doesn't judge us for our circumstances or our choices. His love is constant, His presence unyielding—a powerful, eternal reminder of who He is.

We all have a deep desire to be seen. That's why we spend hours scrolling on social media consuming and sharing "relatable content" because it scratches a sacred human need: to be validated, to be understood, to be seen. We yearn for the best and worst of ourselves to be acknowledged and understood.

"I HAVE SEEN GOD. AND I HAVE BEEN SEEN BY THE GOD WHO SEES ALL." - DR. WILDA GAFNEY

As women, we don't have to limit who God can be to us. We can see God, and we can be seen by God. Let's not dismiss Hagar's testimony just because she's a woman. There will always be those who challenge and minimize our encounters with God.

But you are free to name your experience with God. You're free to see Him through your own eyes. Your understanding of God doesn't have to be filtered through the lens of patriarchy or toxic theology. Who is God to you? Who is the God that you see? God spoke directly to Hagar—not to Sarah and not through Abraham. To Hagar. She wasn't just a producer. She wasn't property. She wasn't just taking up space. Hagar was a woman with the capacity to hear and respond to the voice of her Creator.

That's worth celebrating. You are worthy because you, too, can listen to the voice of God.

The Gem Being Dropped:

God doesn't just see your pain—He sees your potential. He sees the fullness of who you are, beyond the roles others have assigned to you. Even when the world overlooks you, when people diminish you, or when life feels like a wilderness, God's eyes are on you. He's not just watching; He's calling you by name, affirming your worth, and reminding you that your story matters. You are more than what you've been through—you are seen, known, and valued by the God who never looks away.

3

MEN AND WOMEN OF GOD CAN EXPLOIT YOUR BODY, AND IT'S NEVER OKAY

"So Abram said to Sarai, 'Indeed your maid is in your hand; do to her as you please.' And when Sarai dealt harshly with her, she fled from her presence." (Genesis 16:6)

Hagar's situation exposes a truth that can be difficult to swallow: people of faith can be instruments of hurt. Motivated by insecurity and societal pressures, Sarai treats Hagar as a means to an end. Despite being blessed by God, Abraham doesn't intervene to protect Hagar. This isn't about painting all religious people with a broad brush, but it is a call to be discerning. A particular issue in the Black church community is the exploitation of the gifts and talents of members of the LGBTQ+ community. We will preach a theology that's harmful and homophobic but still expect them to sing our songs, direct our choirs, and play our instruments. Or, among Black women, there has been much taking advantage of our time, resources, and energy but still not allowing women into crucial leadership positions. Then you have the general idea of paying ministers less in the name of the gospel but exploiting their hard work, long hours, and difficult decisions. This cannot be in the body of Christ.

The harsh reality is that exploitation often hides behind spiritual language. Consider the story of a young woman in her twenties who had a natural talent for administration. Her pastor frequently praised her for her "servant's heart," but that "praise" came with endless demands. She was asked to organize church events, manage finances, and even handle personal errands, all under the guise of serving the kingdom. Over time, her mental health began to decline, and her prayers started sounding like cries for relief rather than joy. She realized that what she was experiencing wasn't ministry—it was manipulation.

The same holds true for situations where women's bodies are exploited through expectations to dress, act, or perform in ways that satisfy a narrow, male-dominated view of what is "godly." From pulpit critiques about modesty to unspoken rules about emotional availability, the burden often falls disproportionately on women. This misuse of power isn't just harmful—it's ungodly. Faith shouldn't be a tool for control but a source of liberation.

Our worship should empower us to treat each other with love and respect, fostering a culture where no one is reduced to a commodity or a tool.

"THE HARSH REALITY IS THAT EXPLOITATION OFTEN HIDES BEHIND SPIRITUAL LANGUAGE."

The Gem Being Dropped

Don't allow anyone, not even someone who claims to be religious, to use your body or emotions for their gain. Listen to your intuition and trust your inner voice. If someone is causing you pain, know you have the strength to walk away.

4

YOU'RE ALLOWED TO LEAVE THE RELATIONSHIP IF IT'S HURTING YOU

> *"And He said, 'Hagar, Sarai's maid, where have you come from, and where are you going?' She said, 'I am fleeing from the presence of my mistress Sarai.' The Angel of the Lord said to her, 'Return to your mistress, and submit yourself under her hand."* (Genesis 16:8,9)

Hagar's journey into the wilderness is a profound act of self-preservation. She courageously decides to leave an emotionally and likely physically abusive situation. While the societal norms of her time might have condemned her for fleeing, her actions speak volumes to us today.

In choosing to leave, Hagar rejects Sarai's abuse, degradation, and the idea that she is merely property to be used. The verb used in Genesis 16:11 to describe Sarai's mistreatment of Hagar is the same one used later to describe the oppression of the Israelites under Egyptian slavery. Her resistance and rejection of that treatment reflect an inner strength and a refusal to accept a life of oppression.

Yet, Hagar returns—not because she is powerless, but because her circumstances demand it. In the wilderness, survival is impossible, especially for a pregnant woman about to give birth. Returning is not a sign of defeat but a strategy for survival.

Sometimes, liberation takes time. Hagar models the wisdom of making choices that protect her life and her child's future, even in the face of exploitation.

You have permission to do the same thing. You are free to make decisions that prioritize your well-being. You are free to choose survival today so you can fight for liberation tomorrow. You are free to resist and reject abuse, even if it takes time to fully step into freedom.

"SOMETIMES, LIBERATION TAKES TIME!"

The Gem Being Dropped:

It takes immense courage to leave a relationship that harms you, but sometimes, it's the most loving thing you can do for yourself. You are worthy of healthy, fulfilling relationships that uplift your spirit. Don't be afraid to walk away from situations that diminish your worth. God has a purpose for your life, and it doesn't begin or end with someone else's happiness.

TIME TO DROP YOUR OWN GEMS

- Have you ever felt pressured to fulfill a specific role or purpose? What gifts, talents, and passions do you feel called to develop and embrace beyond these expectations?
- When have you felt truly "seen" in your life, and how did it impact you? What would it mean for you to believe that God sees and cares about every detail of your story, even the parts that feel hidden or dismissed?
- Have you ever been taken advantage of by people you trusted, especially within your faith community? How can you begin to set boundaries and heal from that pain while keeping your faith intact?
- Reflect on a time when you needed to leave something or someone behind to protect your well-being. What did you learn about your inner strength, and what steps might you take to trust yourself in future decisions?
- Have there been moments where you felt compelled to return

to a difficult situation out of necessity? How do you hold space for both survival and hope for freedom, and what might liberation look like for you in this season?

♦ In what ways have societal or cultural expectations impacted your self-image or sense of worth? How can you begin to define your own values, setting aside others' expectations, to honor your authentic self?

♦ How do you define dignity and respect in your life, and what boundaries do you need to protect these values, especially in relationships and communities that may not see your total worth?

_____

_____

_____

_____

_____

_____

_____

_____

_____

_____

_____

_____

4

LESSONS FROM REBEKAH

Location: Rebekah lived in Paddan-Aram and later moved to Canaan after marrying Isaac (Genesis 24:10; 24:67).

RELATIONSHIP STATUS: MARRIED BY CHOICE

FAST FACTS:

- Rebekah was chosen as Isaac's wife after she offered water to Abraham's servant and his camels at a well, showing her kindness and hospitality (Genesis 24:14-19).
- She is known for helping her son Jacob deceive Isaac to receive the blessing meant for Esau, a move that created family tension (Genesis 27:5-17).
- Rebekah was barren for 20 years before giving birth to twins Esau and Jacob (Genesis 25:21).

LIFE EVENTS:

♦ Rebekah left her family in Paddan-Aram to marry Isaac, and they settled in Canaan (Genesis 24:58-67).

♦ She struggled with barrenness for 20 years but finally conceived after Isaac prayed to the Lord (Genesis 25:21).

♦ While pregnant, she received a prophecy that her two sons would become two nations, and the elder would serve the younger (Genesis 25:23).

♦ Rebekah favored Jacob over Esau and helped him deceive Isaac into giving him the blessing meant for Esau, which caused a lasting family divide (Genesis 27:5-17).

THE WOMEN WHO CAN RELATE:

♦ Women who've left their homeland or family behind, stepping into unfamiliar environments for love, family, or opportunity.

♦ Women who've experienced seasons of waiting, particularly around deeply personal desires like conceiving or building something meaningful.

♦ Women who've navigated the complexities of favoritism in family dynamics, whether as a parent, sibling, or child.

♦ Women who've felt the weight of making decisions that challenge norms but have far-reaching impacts on their family or relationships.

- Women who've been praised or judged for using their intelligence and initiative to navigate complicated family or relationship situations.

- Women who've grappled with societal or religious expectations around marriage and relationships, striving to align with God's will while staying true to themselves.

- Women who long for love but wrestle with emotional walls built from past hurts, desiring healing and the vulnerability to love fully again.

She's a phenomenal woman tucked away in the book of Genesis, often overshadowed by Sarah's drama and Rachel and Leah's scandalous antics. But Rebekah's story is bursting with wisdom for women like us, navigating love, sex, and relationships in a world that can feel awfully judgmental.

Now, Rebekah gets a bad rap sometimes. Some folks paint her as a manipulative schemer, while others see her as a victim of her circumstances. But Rebekah's story is far more complex than those one-dimensional takes. Like us, we'll see a woman who grapples with love, faith, and societal pressures. Through it all, she emerges as a woman who makes choices, uses her gifts, and ultimately finds her own path within a patriarchal system.

1

WOMEN CAN RUN THINGS, TOO

"Then the young woman ran and told her mother's household about these things." Genesis 24:28 (NRSV)

After Rebekah meets Abraham's servant by the well, the Bible says she runs to her mother's house. That's an exciting detail that suggests she comes from a matriarchal family. Dr. Wilda Gafney writes in her book The Womanist Midrash, "Her father identifies himself with a maternal name in Genesis 24:15 and 24 as Bethuel ben Milcah, Bethuel, the son of Milcah, his mother, the niece and sister-in-law of Sarah and Abraham." It's a reminder that women are capable and worthy of leading families across generations. We see this in several tribes and nations in African countries, where women are actually in charge and highly respected. Even in nature, we see female leadership and authority being demonstrated. Orca whales have a matrilineal structure where the female whales are in charge, setting the trails or courses the whales in their family will take. It's a reminder that it was never God's intent to declare that men must automatically rule or control women.

The fact that Rebekah, a woman of status and from the family of Abraham, comes from a matriarchal family shows that God values the leadership and dominion of women. This doesn't mean that we don't need men, nor does it imply fierce independence to our detriment. But it does mean that between the lines of scripture, there are women who come from families where women—not men—lead and lead well. Rebekah was a blessed woman. She had flaws, but being raised in a woman-focused household did not leave her with deficiencies. God honors and needs it. I'm so glad Rebekah ran to her mommy's house.

The Gem Being Dropped:

Women can step into leadership roles. Do not minimize, reject, or despise women who lead.

2.

YOU STILL GET TO CHOOSE, EVEN IF GOD IS INVOLVED

"So they said, 'We will call the young woman and ask her personally.' Then they called Rebekah and said to her, 'Will you go with this man?' And she said, 'I will go.'" (Genesis 24:57-58)

"Delight yourself also in the Lord, and He shall give you the desires of your heart." (Psalm 37:4)

While Rebekah's family consults her, the power dynamic leans toward her future husband's family. However, the fact that they asked her suggests some agency in choosing her path. Coming from a family where women's voices are respected and elevated made it easier for Rebekah to make decisions that honored her desires. I love that the family checked in with her to see if she wanted to marry this man. This can be seen as a fight for a voice in a patriarchal system, but it's also a testament to the power of being entrenched in environments where women have power, autonomy, and freedom.

This might be surprising, considering Rebekah's whole story

revolves around a divinely orchestrated marriage. Truthfully, God may nudge us in a specific direction, but He doesn't force us down the aisle. There's a pervasive mindset in Christian circles that suggests God has only one person for you to marry. For God to give us only one person to marry out of billions of people would negate our freedom to choose, which is a hallmark of God's character. God will never force us to do something. He will never make you marry someone against your will. God may make suggestions, guide us, provide us with wisdom, give us spirit-led intuition, and send people who love us to offer Godly guidance, but at the end of the day, we still have to make a choice.

Many women blame God for their broken marriages because they were under the impression that God told them they had to marry their partner. This thinking absolves partners of their responsibility in making marriages work. Even if God's will is breathing on a marriage prospect, we still have a massive responsibility to make decisions supporting a healthy marriage. It's not simply, "God told me to marry this man, so it's definitely going to work out." That's not how it works. Rebekah's marriage worked because it was a decision, not a demand.

Rebekah's story gives women permission to choose who they marry. More than being concerned about being chosen, ask yourself if you would choose to marry that man. Ask yourself if this is what you desire. Yes, God may have orchestrated a divine love encounter, but God still honors your desire to choose who you want to marry.

And the grace of God is so outrageous and unique that God can bless another God-ordained relationship if you choose not to be with another Godly man for any reason.

Purity culture drilled the idea into our brains that there could be only one person and that we needed to date, court, or marry only that one person. While there are stories where this has happened, understand that God works in a multiplicity of ways and doesn't decrease the favor and love He manifests in your relationships. Many women carry shame into their marriages because they feel like they're settling for a second marriage or are divorced. Or they feel like it can't be God's best because their partner has had multiple relationships, or they've had several themselves. Purity culture focuses on perfection more than on the favor, mercy, and grace of God.

Remember, Rebekah wasn't coerced. The servant describes Isaac's qualities, and Rebekah's family seeks her consent before she leaves for a new land. She had a choice, and she said yes. Listen to your gut, girl! Trust your instincts when it comes to love.

"REBEKAH'S MARRIAGE WORKED BECAUSE IT WAS A DECISION, NOT A DEMAND."

The Gem Being Dropped:

Sis, even in a world obsessed with aligning with God's will, your intuition and desires matter. Don't be afraid to say no to a relationship that doesn't feel right, even if it seems preordained. God respects your agency, and so should your partner.

3

KINDNESS AND GENEROSITY
ARE SUPERPOWERS

"And when she had finished giving him a drink, she said, 'I will draw water for your camels also, until they have finished drinking.' Then she quickly emptied her pitcher into the trough, ran back to the well to draw water, and drew for all his camels." (Genesis 24:19-20)

"The generous soul will be made rich, and he who waters will also be watered himself." (Proverbs 11:25)

Rebekah fed a considerable number of camels. This wasn't just a cup of water. Rebekah served several camels, drawing hundreds of gallons from the well. Can you see her dusty, well-manicured feet going back and forth, serving camels for a man she just met? The sun is high in the sky, she's sweaty, and she has her own agenda to tend to, but she takes time to quench the thirst of this gentleman and his camels. Rebekah teaches us that sometimes, blessings come disguised as hard work. Her act of kindness, dressed in hard work, opened doors.

Be open to opportunities to be generous and kind, even when they seem unexpected or require going above and beyond. It's admirable to cultivate a heart of generosity—not to find a man, but because it's a superpower that brings the kingdom of God into dark and dreary places.

Ultimately, this is what God desires for us. So no, I don't want us falling over ourselves to serve a random man a drink, carry his bags, or be ostentatiously generous to prove our worth or earn love. I want Rebekah and us to cultivate a heart of generosity, not to win a man, but because it's a significant value for ourselves. Proverbs 11:25 speaks about what happens when you're generous. "A generous person will prosper; whoever refreshes others will be refreshed." The word "generous" is associated with being a blessing—a gift. The idea is that someone who blesses others will "drench" or soak them in generosity. You make sure they're good—like really good—because of your generous heart. And a person who blesses others with gifts will grow fat, prospering both physically and spiritually.

The Bible describes Rebekah as strikingly beautiful, but her story emphasizes something just as valuable: her acts of service. We see her offering water to the weary traveler (who happens to be Isaac's servant) without being asked, even extending her hospitality to his camels. This act of kindness sets the wheels of her destiny in motion.

The Gem Being Dropped:

While beauty privilege is real, genuine kindness and a willingness to serve leave a lasting impression. Focus on cultivating a heart of generosity and using your gifts to uplift others. That kind of inner beauty is a magnet for healthy relationships.

4

HE BETTER SHOWER YOU WITH GIFTS AND APPRECIATION! IT'S OKAY TO DESIRE A GENEROUS PARTNER.

"So it was, when the camels had finished drinking, that the man took a golden nose ring weighing half a shekel, and two bracelets for her wrists weighing ten shekels of gold." (Genesis 24:22)

Sis. The servant dropped bangles, nose rings, and gold in her lap. This wasn't love bombing. It was a generous man showering a woman with gifts because he appreciated who she was and what she did. It's okay to want a gracious man in the dating process and in your relationships with men. It's okay to choose to surround yourself with men who are naturally in the business of flooding you with gifts of appreciation and adoration.

You do not have to settle for a frugal, stingy man who's reluctant to lay it on thick for you. Some men are generous with their time, resources, and energy and would revel in the opportunity to uplift and encourage you with their generosity. Just for being you. Just for being the amazing woman that you are. You don't have to earn affection and adoration from men. Just show up as yourself.

There's also much healing in our hearts that needs to happen so we can readily receive generous, expensive, over-the-top gifts from men. From an early age, we're taught to associate generous men with ulterior motives, thinking they want something in return. I used to believe this, too. But we must realize that not every generous act comes with strings attached. Yes, God calls us to be discerning, but we should also heal from the brokenness that prevents us from accepting men's generosity. We must examine the societal structures that create fear and anxiety around men being kind.

Ultimately, Rebekah shows us the way forward. She permits us to be open to receiving, not to earn the favor of a man, but to be open to being blessed by him. And there's nothing wrong with that.

The Gem Being Dropped:

Receiving kindness and generosity isn't selfish; it's part of a healthy relationship dynamic. Don't settle for less—value yourself enough to seek a partner who honors you with kindness and appreciation.

5

VIRGIN SHAMING ISN'T COOL

"Now the young woman was very beautiful to behold, a virgin; no man had known her. And she went down to the well, filled her pitcher, and came up." (Genesis 24:16)

The text says she was a virgin, or said another way, she lacked sexual experience. Perspectives around not having sexual experience in your 20s, 30s, and 40s are slowly shifting. However, there is still residue that makes women who are virgins feel wrong or silly for not having sexual experience. Virgin shaming is the evil twin of slut shaming. It's about making women feel bad for lacking sexual encounters in their history of relationships. Some women hold on to their V-card but also carry shame and regret with it. Men have made women feel bad for waiting, often saying things like, "What are you waiting for? How long are you going to wait? You're not going to find a perfect man to have sex with. You might as well give it up." Part of the reason women feel ashamed about being virgins is due to the societal expectation that you'll lose it by a certain age. Our culture puts a lot of pressure on having sex at a young age—almost as much as having your first drink or getting your driver's license. Add to this the purity culture overtones, and you get plenty of shame if you have a sexual encounter outside of marriage. It's like you're damned if you do or don't.

Thankfully, Rebekah frees us from that shame and criticism. She reminds us that our worth and confidence can stand firm on whose family we're part of, our values, and even our beauty. Your worth does not need to be rooted in your body count. I also want to acknowledge that the term "virgin" is problematic, but I will use it because it's still a popular term. Virginity is a social construct more than an actual thing; it was created to control the bodies of women. A healthier term would be "sexually inexperienced" or "awaiting one's sexual debut." But the word "virgin" is loaded. Still, my focus in this section is to highlight that making fun of women like Rebekah, who are sexually inactive, is never okay. Movies like The 40-Year-Old Virgin and others have made a point of mocking sexually inexperienced people as something to be laughed at or overcome as if it's a problem. Social media can also be a hotbed for cruel comments and shaming directed at those perceived as sexually inexperienced. While men may be praised for their sexual conquests, women are often shamed or labeled negatively for similar behavior. But then, at the same time, they're treated as less than innocent or childish for not having sexual experiences.

There are also issues around relationships with people who have had sexual encounters. Some women want a man who is also sexually inexperienced like them, while others prefer a man who has had sex before. What should be of primary concern is their ability to communicate, their ability to love you, and their willingness to grow together in loving each other sexually, regardless of what's happened in their sexual past. Priorities should center around mental, emotional, and sexual health more than insisting on a partner with a specific body count. If a man has conquered several female bodies, that doesn't mean he will know a thing about pleasuring yours. Your body is unique and will require a man who is willing to learn and understand who you are. So there's no need to be ashamed of your sexual inexperience with a man because what's most important is the love, care, and affection one has for each other. Honor your values and also be aware that a man who's not a virgin can love you deeply, even if you are. Removing shame from your sexual decisions is crucial because carrying shame into the bedroom will make it increasingly difficult to be vulnerable and open with your partner. A sad outcome of virgin shaming is vaginismus, a condition where women are unable to be penetrated due to tension, making penetration painful and uncomfortable. The shame attached to virginity will make it hard to open up physically and emotionally during sexual encounters.

"IF A MAN HAS CONQUERED SEVERAL FEMALE BODIES, THAT DOESN'T MEAN HE WILL KNOW A THING ABOUT PLEASURING YOURS!"

The Gem Being Dropped

Let's dismantle the myth that a woman's worth is tied to her sexual history. Our value comes from who we are, not what we've done or haven't done in the bedroom. Shame has no place in our pursuit of love and healthy relationships. You don't have to compare yourself to other women to feel good about yourself.

6

NOT ALL PREGNANCIES ARE DESIRED OR HAPPY OCCASIONS

"But the children struggled together within her, and she said, 'If all is well, why am I like this?' So she went to inquire of the Lord." (Genesis 25:22)

We're slowly seeing a shift in how women feel about admitting they don't want children. However, there's still plenty of shame and negativity around a woman not having a traditional, joyous experience around having and raising children. There are women who, if they could do it over again, would think twice about having children, even though they love them dearly. It's harsh but true. Sometimes, women felt it was their duty as women to bring a child into the world, even if it wasn't on their to-do list.

I have a friend who knew early in her 20s that she had no desire to have children. The questions, concerns, and outright contempt she has received because of her decision not to have children are wild. On the flip side, women who don't have children often receive pity or sad looks. I bring this up because Rebekah had a tough pregnancy, and she cried out to God, asking why this was happening to her.

Rebekah's response to a difficult pregnancy gives women of God the freedom to be honest about childbearing experiences that were less than desirable.

Rebekah's experience also highlights the physical and emotional challenges women face during pregnancy. We often focus on the two baby boys fighting in her womb because it foreshadows the two powerful nations that will arise from them. But we overlook that the boxing ring for this fight was Rebekah's womb. It wasn't fun or pretty, and it was painful and arduous. The text doesn't mention if Rebekah even wanted children. Isaac is the one who prayed, not her.

Here are seven reasons why some women might have negative experiences with pregnancy and childbirth or why they may not desire to have children in the first place:

- ◆ Physical Discomfort and Pain: Pregnancy and childbirth can be physically demanding and uncomfortable. Women may experience morning sickness, back pain, fatigue, and other symptoms. Childbirth itself can be a painful, traumatic experience.

- ◆ Mental Health Challenges: Pregnancy and childbirth can trigger or worsen mental health conditions such as anxiety, depression, and postpartum depression. These conditions can significantly impact a woman's well-being and ability to bond with her baby.

- ◆ Loss of Control and Autonomy: Some women feel a loss of control over their bodies and lives during pregnancy and childbirth. They may feel they are not in control of their own decisions or experiences.

- Fear of the Unknown: Pregnancy and childbirth can be scary and unpredictable. Women may fear complications, pain, or the unknown challenges of motherhood.
- Societal and Cultural Pressures: Many women feel societal pressure to have children, even if they don't desire them. This pressure can come from family, friends, or cultural norms.
- Financial Concerns: Raising a child is expensive. Some women may feel that they cannot afford to have children or would have to sacrifice their financial goals and dreams.
- Lack of Support: Women without robust support systems may find it harder to cope with the challenges of pregnancy, childbirth, and motherhood.

It's important to note that these are just a few potential reasons why some women may have negative experiences with pregnancy and childbirth or why they may not desire to have children. Every woman's experience is unique, and many other factors can influence her decisions and feelings about motherhood.

It's essential to respect the choices of women who do not want to have children. There is no one-size-fits-all answer to motherhood, and every woman has the right to make decisions about her body and life.

The Gem Being Dropped:

Motherhood doesn't look the same for everyone, and it's okay to acknowledge the challenges. God sees you in all experiences and validates your feelings, whether joyful or painful.

7

LOVE IS A BEAUTIFUL THING

"Then Isaac brought her into his mother Sarah's tent; and he took Rebekah and she became his wife, and he loved her. So Isaac was comforted after his mother's death." (Genesis 24:67)

"There is no fear in love; but perfect love casts out fear, because fear involves torment. But he who fears has not been made perfect in love." (1 John 4:18)

Sylvie's Love: Set in the 1950s, this film tells the story of a young woman who reunites with her first love after he returns from the army. It explores themes of dreams, aspirations, and unwavering love. Not without imperfections or issues, it's a beautiful story of love. Similarly, Rebekah's story, though not explicitly romantic, suggests a loving bond that provides a counterpoint to the transactional aspects of arranged marriage. It's a reminder to release our jaded perspectives about love and relationships that hold us back from experiencing true love. The Bible talks about having a stubborn heart exchanged for a heart of flesh. (Ezekiel 36:26,27) The word stubborn used there is building up walls. It gives this idea that a stubborn heart is unyielding because it holds walls around its heart to protect itself from experiencing pain and heartbreak. There are many women of God with stubborn hearts regarding love and relationships. We have put walls around the idea of growing in love again because of what happened to us. We don't think we can experience love because we're either too old, too young, too busy, too independent, too vital, too weak, too spiritual, and the list of reasons goes on. But the bible says Isaac loved Rebekah. There was a real connection there. I want us to believe that if you want it, there's an Isaac for you, too—a man who will love and cherish you. Ask the Holy Spirit to melt your stubborn heart around love, even if it requires therapy. Love is beautiful, and we all deserve an Isaac in our lives. Isaac wasn't perfect, but he loved Rebekah perfectly. Would it be the same for all of us?

The Gem Being Dropped:

Love is real and powerful. Don't let past hurts keep you from embracing love with an open heart. Trust that God can bring healing and the right person into your life at the right time.

TIME TO DROP YOUR OWN GEMS:

- Have you ever felt pressured to choose your family or relationships that caused conflict? How did that decision impact you, and what would you do differently today?

- Rebekah came from a family that valued women's voices. What messages about women's leadership and autonomy did you grow up with, and how have they shaped how you see yourself today? What values do you want to embrace or change in your journey of empowerment?

- Rebekah was not coerced into marriage but was given the chance to choose.

- Think about a relationship or major life decision: were you clear about what you wanted, or did external pressures influence you? How can you become more intentional about aligning your choices with your desires?

- The Bible praises Rebekah's kindness and generosity, which shaped her journey.

- How do you express kindness and generosity in your own life, and how can you cultivate a heart of service not to prove worth but to share your authentic self?

- Rebekah's pregnancy was complex and painful, and she turned to God for understanding. Have you experienced moments of inner struggle where you needed answers or clarity? What practices or people help you find peace, especially when facing challenges in areas others may assume are joyful?

- Rebekah's story shows that love can provide healing and comfort. Are there walls you've built around love and relationships due to past experiences? What steps, big or small, can you take to soften those walls and allow yourself to believe in the possibility of healthy, lasting love?

- Rebekah received valuable gifts as a sign of honor and respect. How do you feel about receiving kindness and generosity from others, especially in relationships? Do you hold beliefs that might limit your ability to receive love and support fully?

_____

_____

_____

_____

_____

_____

_____

_____

_____

_____

_____

_____

5

LESSONS
FROM
RACHEL &
LEAH

Location: Rachel and Leah lived in the region of Haran, in Mesopotamia, where their father, Laban, resided. Later, they moved with Jacob and his family to Canaan. (Genesis 29:4-6, Genesis 31:17-18, Genesis 33:18)

RELATIONSHIP STATUS: SISTER WIVES

FAST FACTS:

- Rachel was a shepherdess when Jacob first met her (Genesis 29:9), which was considered unconventional for women at that time.

- Leah was described as having "weak eyes," which some interpret to mean she was less attractive than Rachel (Genesis 29:17).

- When Jacob fled with his family, Rachel stole her father's household gods (idols), which led to a confrontation with Laban (Genesis 31:19).

- Leah became the mother of six sons, including Judah, from whom the line of King David and, ultimately, Jesus descended (Genesis 35:23).

♦ Rachel died giving birth to her second son, Benjamin, and was buried near Bethlehem (Genesis 35:19-20).

LIFE EVENTS:

♦ Jacob fell in love with Rachel and agreed to work for seven years to marry her, but Laban deceived him into marrying Leah first (Genesis 29:18-25).

♦ Leah struggled for Jacob's love, giving birth to several sons, while Rachel faced the pain of infertility (Genesis 29:31-30:1).

♦ Rachel finally bore a son, Joseph, after years of infertility, and he would go on to play a significant role in saving the family (Genesis 30:22-24).

♦ The rivalry between Rachel and Leah became so intense that they gave their maidservants to Jacob to bear children on their behalf (Genesis 30:1-13).

♦ Rachel died in childbirth while giving birth to her second son, Benjamin, leaving a profound impact on Jacob and the family (Genesis 35:16-19).

THE WOMEN WHO CAN RELATE:

♦ Women who have experienced the pain of being in a competitive or difficult relationship, especially with friends, colleagues, siblings, or in marriage.

- Women who have felt unloved or overlooked but have found their identity or strength in other ways.
- Women who have struggled with infertility or the desire to have children.
- Women who've dealt with family manipulation or complicated dynamics.
- Women who have daddy issues that affect their love life.
- Women who have strained relationships with their father.
- Women who have had to reconcile feelings of jealousy and insecurity, especially in relationships where comparison seems unavoidable.
- Women who have felt less than from their boyfriend or spouse.
- Women who don't feel beautiful.
- Women who don't feel loved.

Sisters, rivals, mothers of Israel—the stories of Rachel and Leah in Genesis are far more profound than a sad story of jealousy. By the end of this chapter, I hope you see them not just as Biblical figures but as real women navigating a patriarchal culture with lessons that resonate deeply with generations of women.

This exploration dives into the hearts of Rachel and Leah, unveiling how their struggles with comparison, manipulation, self-worth, and father wounds offer powerful messages for today's modern women of faith.

STOP COMPARING YOUR BODY WITH OTHERS:

"Leah's eyes were delicate, but Rachel was beautiful in form and appearance." (Genesis 29:17)

"For we dare not class ourselves or compare ourselves with those who commend themselves. But they, measuring themselves by themselves, and comparing themselves among themselves, are not wise." (2 Corinthians 10:12)

"I will praise You, for I am fearfully and wonderfully made; marvelous are Your works, and that my soul knows very well." (Psalm 139:14)

I love my parents' flower garden. Each flower is unique: Some are tall and elegant, like lilies, and others are short and vibrant, like pansies. Some have bold, colorful blooms, while others have delicate, fragrant ones. They all have their beauty and purpose in the garden.

Now, imagine one of the flowers in the garden (let's say a daisy) feeling insecure because it sees a rose with a larger, more dramatic bloom. The daisy starts to focus on its perceived shortcomings, wishing it were taller or more colorful. This comparison steals the daisy's joy and takes away its energy to grow and thrive in its way.

I bring up the flowers in my parents' garden because the Bible describes Rachel as beautiful, while Leah is said to have "weak eyes" (Genesis 29:17). Two different flowers grow in the same garden. This has often been interpreted as Leah being unattractive. However, another perspective suggests that "weak eyes" could symbolize a lack of societal status or social power. Beauty standards of the time likely favored youthful features and fertility. Rachel likely embodied these ideals. Imagine the pressure Leah must have felt, constantly measured against her sister's dazzling exterior. Regardless of what "weak eyes" means, the story highlights the dangers of comparison. Both sisters fall prey to societal beauty standards, creating a rift in their relationship and fueling their competition for Jacob's affection.

We, too, need help with comparing our bodies to impossible standards. When we compare ourselves, it creates unrealistic ideals in our minds. Many social media portrayals and beauty standards are like the "perfect rose"—heavily edited and unattainable for most. Embrace that you have a unique body that God created just for you. Like each flower has its charm, every woman's body has unique strengths and features. Comparison overshadows this individuality. Focusing on what others have can lead to feelings of inadequacy like the daisy feeling inferior to the rose. The daisy forgets its beauty by fixating on the rose. Similarly, comparing bodies takes away from celebrating what you love about yourself. Rachel and Leah remind us to celebrate our unique beauty and worth, which goes far beyond physical appearance.

The Gem Being Dropped:

Your worth isn't defined by a number on the scale or someone else's opinion. Embrace your unique beauty and avoid using your energy to compare yourself to others.

2

NOT ALL MEN WHO SLEEP WITH YOU, LOVE YOU. BUT YOU'RE STILL WORTHYOF LOVE WHEN HE DIDN'T LOVE YOU BACK.

"Now it came to pass in the evening, that he took Leah his daughter and brought her to Jacob; and he went in to her. And Laban gave his maid Zilpah to his daughter Leah as a maid. So it came to pass in the morning, that behold, it was Leah. And he said to Laban, 'What is this you have done to me? Was it not for Rachel that I served you? Why then have you deceived me?" (Genesis 29:23-25)

"Since you were precious in My sight, you have been honored, and I have loved you; therefore I will give men for you, and people for your life." (Isaiah 43:4)

"THIS STORY REMINDS US TO LOVE OURSELVES ABOVE ALL THINGS, EVEN WHEN THE MEN WE THOUGHT LOVED US DIDN'T LOVE US BACK!"

"But God demonstrates His own love toward us, in that while we were still sinners, Christ died for us." (Romans 5:8)

"How precious is Your lovingkindness, O God! Therefore the children of men put their trust under the shadow of Your wings." (Psalm 36:7)

Whew, this one barely requires an explanation, but I will dig in. This is not an indictment against you if you've slept with someone who proclaimed love for you but really didn't. That means you're human. There's also no judgment for women who slept with men who blatantly told you they weren't into you. We all have our stories. Trust me.

First, I want us to know that your capacity to love someone who didn't love you speaks to your capacity to love and be loved. It shows your humanity. I want you to take your power back regardless of your story. Be mindful that not all men want to be with you because they love and adore you. Some want to get laid. And sometimes, women want that, too. Again, there is no judgment. What matters most is that we honor God and ourselves with whatever decisions we make with our bodies going forward.

Jacob, bless his heart, was smitten with Rachel. He worked seven long years for her hand in marriage, only to be tricked by Laban, Leah's father, into marrying Leah first! Ouch. Deception and betrayal – not exactly the recipe for happily ever after. This act of manipulation by both men highlights the vulnerability of women in a society that prioritizes male dominance.

While Jacob eventually loves Leah, his initial attraction to Rachel is based on physical beauty.

This story reminds us to love ourselves above all things, even when the men we thought loved us didn't love us back. True love goes beyond physical attraction and should be built on mutual respect, communication, and shared values. Marriage customs also differed back then. Fathers often arranged marriages based on economic or social gain. Love wasn't always the primary factor. This left women like Leah vulnerable to being pawns in their families' schemes. But if Leah were here today, I think she would want us to learn from her story and choose, when possible, to make and own our sexual decisions from a place of power and strength. She would want us to feel and know we are worthy of love, adoration, and affection from a man who loves us wholeheartedly.

The Gem Being Dropped:

You are worthy of love. Period. Love isn't just about physical intimacy. It's about respect, communication, and a deep connection. And you deserve all of that, truly. Don't settle for a relationship that leaves you feeling used or undervalued. Know your worth, queen!

3

YOU'RE MORE THAN WHAT YOU CAN PRODUCE

"Now when Rachel saw that she bore Jacob no children, Rachel envied her sister, and said to Jacob, 'Give me children, or else I die!' And Jacob's anger was aroused against Rachel, and he said, 'Am I in the place of God, who has withheld from you the fruit of the womb?'"
(Genesis 30:1-2)

"When the LORD saw that Leah was unloved, He opened her womb; but Rachel was barren." (Genesis 29:31)

One of my favorite sermons to preach is 'The Battle of the Bellies.' Rachel and Leah went head-to-head in a baby bump competition, each trying to one-up the other in their ability to bear children. And as wild as it sounds, that spirit of competition is alive and well today—it just looks different. It may not be a battle of the bellies, but ladies are found competing with each other based on what we can "produce" often. We look at how many children one has and wonder if we can do the same. We look at where a woman is in life and try to

129

produce the same fruit on our timeline. We peer over one woman's progress in her physical health, and we wish we could produce the same amount of progress as her. It's exhausting. It's like a never-ending race of "what have you produced?"

Now, Leah's initial struggle with infertility speaks to the societal pressure women face to bear children. Her self-worth seems to be tied to her ability to conceive. However, God opens her womb, and she becomes the mother of several sons who become prominent tribes of Israel. Both Rachel and Leah desperately desired to bear children, especially sons, for Jacob. Barrenness was a source of shame and insecurity in their culture. Rachel cried out, "Give me children, or I shall die!" (Genesis 31:16). Leah, after giving birth to four sons, pleaded with God, "Open my womb..." (Genesis 29:31).

This struggle reminds us of a crucial truth: our worth is not measured by what we can produce. This isn't just about children. Maybe your "battle of the bellies" is about achieving as many degrees as possible, building a business empire, or constantly showing off the latest perfect meal or outfit. But God didn't create us to exhaust ourselves trying to live up to impossible standards. Whether or not we meet those standards, our value remains untouched and unshaken.

Always remember your value is high simply because you exist. Nothing more, nothing less.

"ALWAYS REMEMBER YOUR VALUE IS HIGH SIMPLY BECAUSE YOU EXIST."

The Gem Being Dropped

Your value doesn't depend on producing children, accomplishments, or accolades. You're a whole, complete person worthy of love and respect, regardless of family status, career, or anything you "produce." God's love for you is unwavering and unconditional (Romans 8:38-39). If you're struggling with infertility, remember that your worth goes beyond motherhood, and you're not alone. Seek support from those who love you, explore your options, and hold fast to the truth that you're already complete.

DADDY ISSUES CAN AFFECT YOUR LOVE LIFE IF YOU LET THEM

"Then Rachel and Leah answered and said to him, 'Is there still any portion or inheritance for us in our father's house? Are we not considered strangers by him? For he has sold us, and also completely consumed our money." (Genesis 31:14-15)

"And you, fathers, do not provoke your children to wrath, but bring them up in the training and admonition of the Lord." (Ephesians 6:4)

"When my father and my mother forsake me, then the LORD will take care of me." (Psalm 27:10)

A 2018 study published in the Journal of Divorce & Remarriage found that women with unresolved father wounds are more likely to report difficulty trusting men and have a higher risk of experiencing abusive relationships. Let's take a look at some examples that might feel familiar.

Let's call her Successful Susy. She is a high-powered business woman with a distant father who was emotionally unavailable throughout her childhood. She craved his approval but never felt like she could measure up. Now, in her adult relationships, she tends to attract partners who are emotionally distant or workaholics, mirroring her father's behavior. This creates a dynamic where she constantly strives for their approval but feels perpetually unfulfilled.

The People Pleaser Paula grew up with a critical father who constantly put her down. To avoid his disapproval, Paula became a people pleaser, prioritizing others' needs over her own. Now, in her romantic relationships, she struggles to set boundaries and often finds herself in relationships with partners who are demanding or take advantage of her kindness.

The Commitment-Phobe Carissa's father left the family when she was young. This experience instilled a deep fear of abandonment in Carissa. Now, as an adult, she avoids commitment in her relationships, fearing that her partners will eventually leave her, just like her father did.

Rachel and Leah know this story well. They both had a strained relationship with their father, Laban, who deceived and manipulated them. Laban wasn't exactly the Father of the Year— he favored Rachel, used both daughters for his gain, and cared little about their happiness. This fractured relationship with their father likely affected Rachel and Leah's sense of self-worth and created an unhealthy competition for Jacob's love.

In those days, a father's influence held tremendous weight. For Rachel and Leah, this lack of a stable paternal bond may have left them emotionally bruised, impacting their relationships and sense of value. Thankfully, recognizing these wounds is the first step toward healing. We all carry some emotional baggage from our pasts, and it's expected that these patterns will resurface in our adult relationships. Identifying these issues can give us the power to break free from old cycles, build healthier connections, and choose partners who honor and support us.

The Gem Being Dropped:

We can't change our pasts, but we can control how they affect our future. If you notice a pattern of attracting unavailable partners or repeating relationship struggles, seek help to dig into those roots and heal. Let go of any shame or guilt and know that you are worthy of the love that lifts you, not the love that leaves you wanting.

TIME TO DROP YOUR OWN GEMS

- How do you define beauty? What are some ways you can celebrate your unique beauty?

- How does societal pressure around motherhood or family planning impact you? How can you cultivate a sense of self-worth beyond your ability to have children?

- How do societal beauty standards impact your self-worth? How can you challenge these standards and celebrate your unique beauty?

- Have you ever been in a relationship where you felt used or unloved? What are some of the red flags to watch out for?

- How does your self-worth connect to your achievements or relationships?

- Have you ever struggled with comparing yourself to others? What are some strategies you can use to cultivate self-acceptance?

♦ Do you think you have unresolved wounds from your relationship with your father figure? If so, how might this be impacting
your relationships?

6

LESSONS FROM TAMAR

Location: Tamar lived in Canaan, part of the ancient Near East, where Judah and his family resided (Genesis 38)

RELATIONSHIP STATUS: WIDOWED

FAST FACTS:

- Tamar dressed as a prostitute to deceive Judah, her father-in-law, into fulfilling his duty to provide an heir after he failed to give her his third son in marriage (Genesis 38:14-19).
- She gave birth to twins Perez and Zerah through Judah. Perez became part of the genealogical line leading to King David and, ultimately, Jesus (Genesis 38:27-30; Matthew 1:3).

LIFE EVENTS:

- Tamar's first husband, Er, died because he was wicked in the eyes of God (Genesis 38:7).
- Judah's second son, Onan, refused to give Tamar children, so God struck him down as well (Genesis 38:9-10).
- Tamar took matters into her own hands by disguising herself and tricking Judah into impregnating her, securing her rightful place, and ensuring her survival (Genesis 38:13-19).
- Tamar was nearly condemned to death for pregnancy outside of marriage, but when she revealed Judah's signet and staff as proof of the father, he declared her more righteous than he was (Genesis 38:24-26).

THE WOMEN WHO CAN RELATE:

- Women who have had to fight for justice in a world that has wronged or overlooked them.
- Women who are resourceful and get things accomplished no matter what.
- Women who've faced oppression or abandonment and had to take matters into their own hands to survive.
- Women who feel like their value and worth is diminished because they're childless.

- ◆ Women who've been misjudged or condemned but ultimately proved themselves to be righteous or in the right.
- ◆ Women who understand the pain of being overlooked or denied their rights but who still find a way to secure their future.
- ◆ Women who have been hurt deeply by men.
- ◆ Women who've been caught in complicated family dynamics but still played a significant role in God's larger plan.

Tamar is a woman who gets a bad rap but honestly deserves a standing ovation. Tamar's story unfolds in Genesis 38, a chapter often buried in whispers and judgment. But what if we reframe it through a womanist lens that celebrates our strength and challenges the limitations placed on us?

1

IT WASN'T YOUR FAULT

"But Er, Judah's firstborn, was wicked in the sight of the LORD, and the LORD killed him. And Judah said to Onan, 'Go in to your brother's wife and marry her, and raise up an heir to your brother.' But Onan knew that the heir would not be his; and it came to pass, when he went in to his brother's wife, that he emitted on the ground, lest he should give an heir to his brother. And the thing which he did displeased the LORD; therefore He killed him also." (Genesis 38:6-10)

"The LORD redeems the soul of His servants, and none of those who trust in Him shall be condemned." (Psalm 34:22)

"Do not fear, for you will not be ashamed; neither be disgraced, for you will not be put to shame; for you will forget the shame of your youth, and will not remember the reproach of your widowhood anymore." (Isaiah 54:4)

Tamar enters the scene as a young woman married to Er, Judah's eldest son. But the rug is yanked from under her feet when Er dies. As a widow, tradition dictates that she be given to Onan, the next brother, to fulfill his levirate duty. But Onan, motivated by selfishness, avoids impregnating Tamar. Both Er and Onan are judged harshly by God—not just for their treatment of Tamar but for their wickedness.

Many women feel ashamed and guilty about decisions they didn't make. We carry the weight and burden of others' decisions. One of my House of Women members finally found the courage to file for divorce from her husband. She knew it was necessary because he was abusive and a cheater, but she still felt guilty and ashamed because she believed she was creating a broken home for her children. She felt like she was letting her supporters and friends down. All this guilt and shame, though understandable, should not be carried because she did what she could to survive and endure an unhealthy relationship for such a long time. Now, she's getting the divorce so she can finally be free and heal, but she carries shame about a decision she was forced to make because of her husband's actions.

Or maybe you're like another member who struggled with her confidence and self-worth after discovering her father had another child she didn't know about. The secret, rooted in his infidelity and poor decisions, was not hers to carry, yet she couldn't shake this feeling of shame and low self-confidence.

I could go on and share stories of women carrying shame in their minds and bodies that don't belong to them. Tamar teaches us that when the "Ers and Onans" make poor decisions that affect us, we can choose to be disappointed and sad, but we don't have to walk with our heads held low. You're not the one who needs to walk in shame. It's not your fault if he left. It's not your fault if he cheated. It's not your fault that your parents divorced. It's not your fault you were raped. It's not your fault you were abused. It's not your fault you weren't protected. It's not your fault if he didn't fulfill his vows. It's not your fault when others make decisions that hurt you. It's not your fault. They made the choice, not you. Don't feel shame about it, and may you permit Jesus to be the lifter of your head.

The Gem Being Dropped:

So often, we carry the weight of blame for situations beyond our control. Tamar's story reminds us that sometimes bad things happen and are not our fault. We can release the burden of shame and step into the freedom of God's grace.

2

YOUR SEXUAL DECISIONS DON'T PRECLUDE YOU FROM THE FAMILY OF GOD

"And it was told Tamar, saying, 'Look, your father-in-law is going up to Timnah to shear his sheep.' So she took off her widow's garments, covered herself with a veil and wrapped herself, and sat in an open place which was on the way to Timnah; for she saw that Shelah was grown, and she was not given to him as a wife. When Judah saw her, he thought she was a harlot, because she had covered her face." (Genesis 38:13-16)

"For I am persuaded that neither death nor life, nor angels nor principalities nor powers, nor things present nor things to come, nor height nor depth, nor any other created thing, shall be able to separate us from the love of God which is in Christ Jesus our Lord." (Romans 8:38-39)

> *"Now, therefore, you are no longer strangers and for-eigners, but fellow citizens with the saints and members of the household of God." (Ephesians 2:19)*

Judah, hesitant to lose his youngest son, Shelah, to a levirate marriage, sends Tamar back to her father's house with empty promises. Feeling betrayed and desperate to secure her future and fulfill her purpose as a wife and mother, Tamar takes matters into her own hands. She devises a daring plan, disguising herself as a temple prostitute, and seduces Judah, who unknowingly sleeps with his daughter-in-law. Was it dishonest? Yes. Was it risky? Yes. But was it brilliant and oozing with agency, taking back her power in a powerless situation? Absolutely.

Notice she's not condemned or ostracized from the community, but her bold actions secure her place in the lineage of Jesus. Jesus doesn't gatekeep who gets to be in the family of God. If a woman like Tamar, who made a difficult decision to secure her future, can be included in God's family, may it encourage you to remember that you are more than welcome into the arms of God regardless of what you've done or what's been done to you.

I'm speaking to women who have felt disowned by your families and faith communities because of your tough decisions. Maybe you're a woman who decided to keep the baby instead of aborting it, but now you're labeled as having a child out of wedlock. A woman who gets pregnant outside of wedlock might be disowned, mainly if the family views it as a moral failing or a source of gossip. I need you to know that you, my sister, are more than welcome in the family of God, even if people have written you off.

There may be a woman reading this book who chose to make the difficult decision to cut ties with toxic, dysfunctional family members for the sake of your mental and emotional health. You're being painted as a villain. Family members have stopped calling and inviting you to events because of what you're doing to your parents, siblings, or grandparents. You're seen as disrespectful or disloyal.

Tamar teaches us that women who make difficult decisions about their bodies to protect and honor themselves are still welcome in God's family. You're in good company, sister.

"JESUS DOESN'T GATEKEEP WHO GETS TO BE IN THE FAMILY OF GOD."

The Gem Being Dropped:

God doesn't prevent women who have made tough, unpopular choices from experiencing the love, safety, status, and blessings that come from being in the family of God.

3

YOU'RE ALLOWED TO TAKE UP SPACE AND SPEAK UP FOR YOURSELF

> *"When she was brought out, she sent to her father-in-law, saying, 'By the man to whom these belong, I am with child.' And she said, 'Please determine whose these are—the signet and cord, and staff.' So Judah acknowledged them and said, 'She has been more righteous than I, because I did not give her to Shelah my son.' And he never knew her again."* (Genesis 38:25-26)

> *"The LORD is my light and my salvation; whom shall I fear? The LORD is the strength of my life; of whom shall I be afraid?"* (Psalm 27:1)

Tamar's actions were audacious. She challenged the power dynamics and used her wit and courage to advocate for herself. The truth about Judah and Tamar's encounter emerges when Tamar reveals she's pregnant. Judah, initially enraged, is silenced by the evidence Tamar presents – his signet ring, cord, and staff. His ring signifies financial stability. His cord establishes power, and staff defines his authority. It was like she had taken his credit card, driver's license, and passport. These are things that establish his identity, pedigree, and status. But what I love about Tamar is she doesn't say a word. She doesn't beg or plead for mercy not to be stoned or punished. Instead, she boldly lays out the facts, refusing to be minimized, blamed, or silenced. She allows her decision to speak for her. She allowed the way she showed up to Judah to talk loudly on her behalf.

Sometimes, speaking up for yourself is letting the truth speak for you. There are moments where you must be loud and indignant, and then there are moments where you let your work speak for itself. Let your receipts do the talking. Don't be afraid to take up space by allowing the facts to do the talking. When you're on your job, and people are trying to discredit you, show them the receipts. When your partner is trying to gaslight or guilt trip you about something he did, don't waver. Don't shift. Let the facts speak up for you because you're worthy of being seen. You're worthy of being advocated for. Your story is worthy of being elevated and heard. Don't allow others to dim your light because your truth paints them in a dim light or makes them uncomfortable. It's your truth.

Own it and walk in it.

The Gems Being Dropped:

We are worthy of being heard. Like Tamar, we have a voice and are allowed to use it. Don't be afraid to speak your truth, even when it's uncomfortable. God gave you a voice for a reason – use it with power and grace!

4

SHE IS MORE RIGHTEOUS: HOLD SPACE FOR WOMEN WHO CHOOSE DIFFERENTLY

> *"So Judah acknowledged them and said, 'She has been more righteous than I, because I did not give her to Shelah my son.' And he never knew her again." (Genesis 38:26)*

> *"Bear one another's burdens, and so fulfill the law of Christ." (Galatians 6:2)*

At that time, women were seen as property to be exchanged or inherited. But Tamar's actions were a form of resistance. She reclaimed her body as her own, not something to be bartered. Levirate marriage treated women as vessels for procreation, not individuals with desires or needs. But Tamar disrupts this system. She takes control of her body, using it not for a transaction but to secure her future and fulfill her purpose. Notably, the text suggests Judah recognizes Tamar's agency. He proclaims, "She is more righteous than I, since I did not give her to Shelah my son." (Genesis 38:26)

This is important because I want us to have more compassion for women who use their bodies for sex to secure their futures and help fulfill their purpose. I want us Christian women to hold space on our church pews, bible studies, and choir lofts for women who choose to do this. I want us to imagine a world where women who choose to reclaim their bodies by making decisions about their own bodies can be respected, honored, and valued. Worthy of healthcare, protection, and basic rights as a human being. The days of demonizing women who support themselves financially through their bodies need to be over. Compassion doesn't mean agreement. Holding space doesn't mean agreement. It means choosing to see Tamar in the women around us. How would you treat Tamar today? How would you honor her at your church? Would you invite her to sit next to you? Would you do a nails and brunch date with her? Remember, this is the woman who wound up in the family tree of Jesus. Tamar is making us confront the biases, discomfort, and judgment we hold for women who choose to make way for themselves differently than we do. We may see it as less honorable and deplorable. I understand and want to challenge us to sit with Tamar when we make blanket statements about women who don't always have the privilege to make the same decisions we did.

"THE DAYS OF DEMONIZING WOMEN WHO SUPPORT THEMSELVES FINANCIALLY THROUGH THEIR BODIES NEED TO BE OVER."

The Gem Being Dropped:

Learn to hold space for women who survive in ways that make you uncomfortable, don't make sense, or feel icky. Holding space is not an endorsement of risky behavior. Holding space is about empowering women to reclaim their power and agency. Holding space is saying I see and hear you, and I'm praying for you. It's about seeing their humanity and being compassionate and gracious. Work instead on dismantling the systems and policies in place that produce a need for women to make these tough decisions about their bodies in the first place. What would need to change for a woman not to feel the need even to do that?

TIME TO DROP YOUR OWN GEMS:

- Have you ever felt blamed for a situation beyond your control? How can you release that burden and embrace God's grace?

- How do societal messages about female sexuality make you feel? How can you challenge those messages and embrace your God-given sensuality?

- Have you ever felt you had to shrink your voice to fit in? How can you claim your space and speak your truth with confidence?

- What negative messages have you received about your body? How can you begin to see it as a sacred temple worthy of respect and care?

- How does Tamar's story inspire you to live a more empowered and authentic life in your relationship with God and others?

7

LESSONS FROM POTIPHAR'S WIFE

Location: She lived in Egypt, specifically in the household of Potiphar, an officer of Pharaoh and captain of the guard. (Genesis 39:1)

RELATIONSHIP STATUS: MARRIED

FAST FACTS:

♦ Her name is never mentioned in the Bible; she is known as Potiphar's wife.

♦ She is one of the earliest recorded instances of a false accusation of sexual assault (Genesis 39:12-18).

♦ Her actions set the stage for Joseph's imprisonment, leading to his rise to power in Egypt (Genesis 39:20-23).

LIFE EVENTS:

- She attempted to seduce Joseph, her husband's servant, repeatedly, but he refused her advances due to his loyalty to God and Potiphar (Genesis 39:7-10).
- When Joseph fled from her, leaving his cloak behind, she falsely accused him of trying to assault her, using the cloak as "evidence" (Genesis 39:13-18).
- Her false accusation led to Joseph's imprisonment, though this was part of God's larger plan for Joseph's future (Genesis 39:19-20).

THE WOMEN WHO CAN RELATE:

- Women who are in unhappy marriages
- Women with an absent, preoccupied husband
- Women who like sex but don't get enough of it
- Women who have been tempted to commit adultery
- Women who like younger men
- Women who have abused their power or been in positions of authority and used it for personal gain
- Women who've misled others for selfish reasons or out of frustration from unfulfilled desires
- Women who've been involved in complicated relationships where boundaries were crossed

◆ Women who've witnessed false accusations and their consequences, whether they were involved directly or indirectly

Her name alone sparks images of a homewrecker, a villain in Joseph's story. But is there more to Potiphar's wife than meets the eye? What if there's a hidden story, a hurting sister yearning for connection behind that one-dimensional label? To understand her, we must travel back to ancient Egypt, a land of pyramids, power, and strategic alliances, where women held limited choices and love was rarely a factor in marriage. Imagine Potiphar, a high-ranking official, away on duty, leaving his wife in a sexless cage of isolation and longing. Then, Joseph—a young, captivating servant—enters her life. Beneath the Genesis narrative lies a deeper tale, offering us unexpected lessons on desire, power, and the complexities of human interaction. Let's dive in and unearth the gems hidden in her story.

1

YOU STILL HAVE YOUR OWN IDENTITY

"And it came to pass after these things that his master's wife cast longing eyes on Joseph, and she said, 'Lie with me." (Genesis 39:7)

"But now, thus says the Lord, who created you, O Jacob, and He who formed you, O Israel: 'Fear not, for I have redeemed you; I have called you by your name; you are Mine." (Isaiah 43:1)

So many women know about being referred to as Mr. Smith's wife. Or the pastor's wife. As if you don't have a name, personality, career, or life outside of being a wife. As much as we drag our sister, we do have to pause and consider that all the main male characters are called by their government name, but not her. Unlike the men in the story, the only female figure has no name. It can be seen as dehumanizing and disturbing to have such a crucial part of the story revolve around you, but we don't know your name. A woman may be reading this who feels ignored as if her identity doesn't matter because of who you're connected to. This wife sees you and understands what it feels like to be overlooked. She understands what it feels like to have your identity swallowed up by that of a man. It's important that no matter what role you take, what profession you take on, whether you're a mother, wife, entrepreneur, nurse, etc., at the end of the day, you're still you. Don't lose the essence and foundation of who you are. In my S5 Lifestyle, we delve into the sensual side of ourselves to keep our identity alive and well. It's okay to be called your man's wife, but not to the extent that you lose yourself and don't know who you are anymore.

Here are some possible signs you may be losing yourself in a relationship:

You Can't Remember the Last Time You Did Something Just for You.

When was the last time you did you? Whether it's binge-watching your favorite show, going to brunch with your girls, or taking that solo Target run that turns into a mini therapy session, if your life has become a "we" fest, it's time to check in with yourself.

Your Dreams Are Collecting Dust.

Did you used to talk about starting your own business, learning Spanish, or finally finishing that book you started writing? If those dreams now feel like distant memories, it might be time to dust them off and reintroduce yourself to them.

You Agree with Everything He Says, Even When You Don't.

If you find yourself nodding like a bobblehead just to keep the peace—even when you know deep down you don't agree—sis, your voice deserves to be heard. A relationship is not a dictatorship.

You're Dressing to Impress Him, Not Yourself.

Wearing clothes that he likes instead of outfits that make you feel like Beyoncé on her Renaissance tour? Don't let anyone make you dim your shine. Wear what makes you feel powerful, sexy, and authentically you.

You've Put Your Friendships on the Shelf.

If the group chat has been dry because you're always with him and can't remember the last time you had a girls' night, it's time to revisit your village. Your friendships are just as important as your romantic relationship.

You Don't Recognize Yourself in the Mirror.

It's not just about your looks—it's your spark, your vibe, your essence. If you feel like you've lost your edge or your "thing" that makes you you, it's worth pausing to reconnect with yourself.

You Feel Guilty for Wanting Alone Time.

Wanting a solo coffee run or a few hours to journal is not selfish.

It's healthy. If you feel bad for carving out space for yourself, it's time to reclaim that right unapologetically.

Your Hobbies Are "On Hold."

When was the last time you picked up your paintbrush, guitar, or crochet needles? If all your free time is centered on your partner's interests, it's time to reintroduce yourself to your passions.

You Shrink Yourself to Keep the Peace.

If you're holding back your personality, ideas, or even your laughter to avoid conflict or to fit his expectations, sis, that's not partnership—that's self-erasure. You deserve to take up space.

You Can't Make a Decision Without His Input.

If you can't trust your own judgment anymore, whether about what to order at the restaurant or whether you should take a new job, it's a sign that you need to rebuild your confidence in yourself.

These signs aren't about shaming anyone—they're gentle reminders to keep your identity alive and thriving. A relationship should enhance your life, not consume it.

Yes, there is compromise and growing together, but always know you have the agency to align with your partner in ways that empower and strengthen you rather than deplete or minimize you.

The Gem Being Dropped:

Your identity always matters. Don't lose who you truly are when you partner with your spouse. Your voice, your spark, your you-ness—it all matters. And when you bring your full self to the relationship, you win, and your partner does too.

MANAGE YOUR SEXUAL URGES

"But he refused and said to his master's wife, 'Look, my master does not know what is with me in the house, and he has committed all that he has to my hand. There is no one greater in this house than I, nor has he kept back anything from me but you, because you are his wife. How then can I do this great wickedness, and sin against God?'" (Genesis 39:8-9)

"For this is the will of God, your sanctification: that you should abstain from sexual immorality; that each of you should know how to possess his own vessel in sanctification and honor." (1 Thessalonians 4:3-4)

Some scholars argue that her attempt to seduce Joseph may have stemmed from unmet needs for intimacy, exacerbated by her social isolation and the pressures of being a high-ranking official's wife. The prominent scholar Tikva Frymer-Kensky posits that stories of seduction or enticement involving powerful women, like Potiphar's wife, reveal not just sexual desires but also "the emotional hunger and power struggles that marked ancient households" (Reading the Women of the Bible, 2002). This could support the idea that Potiphar's wife was motivated not merely by physical desire but by a craving for personal connection and agency. Was Potiphar's African wife dealing with a husband who couldn't get it up? We don't know for sure, but let's be clear: this is quite common.

Many women are in sexless marriages not because of the women but because of the man. And because of the stigmas of not coming off as too freaky or slutty, women suffer in silence and keep it to themselves. Erectile dysfunction (ED) affects about 22% of men, with a higher prevalence among Black men (Oxford Academic, 2023). This dysfunction can lead to sexless marriages, causing emotional distress for both partners (Lehmiller, 2023). Despite Potiphar's wife's seemingly strained marriage, women have a responsibility to manage their urges and be responsible with their sex drive. The fact that she was hurting doesn't give any validity to her action of luring Joseph to sleep with her. Sending sexual advances to a man who didn't ask for it is rapey. Consent is always queen, even for women. This is a big one; frankly, it's a challenge for all of us, regardless of the era. When you're going through a difficult, rough season in your marriage or relationship, you must have the maturity to manage your sexual desires in ways that still honor God.

"YOUR DESIRES ARE VALID, BUT YOUR DECISIONS DEFINE YOU."

Gem Being Dropped:

Your desires are valid, but your decisions define you. Don't let unmet needs push you into dishonoring yourself or God. Instead, confront the silence. Speak up, seek help, and reclaim your agency. Healthy intimacy starts with mutual respect, communication, and God's design for wholeness—even when the struggle is real.

3

YOUR HUSBAND IS THERE TO PLEASURE YOU

"Then she spoke to him with words like these, saying, 'The Hebrew servant whom you brought to us came in to me to mock me; so it happened, as I lifted my voice and cried out, that he left his garment with me and fled outside." (Genesis 39:17-18)

"Let the husband render to his wife the affection due her, and likewise also the wife to her husband. The wife does not have authority over her own body, but the husband does. And likewise the husband does not have authority over his own body, but the wife does." (1 Corinthians 7:3-4)

"I am my beloved's, and his desire is toward me." (Song of Solomon 7:10)

Do not let your man off the hook when it comes to your pleasure. Ms. Potiphar went about it all wrong—what she did was predatory, manipulative, and downright sinful. But her story forces us to confront some uncomfortable realities. While she is absolutely responsible for her actions, her situation also speaks to the broader issues at play: unmet needs, neglect, and the imbalance of power within her marriage.

It's clear that Potiphar's household wasn't flourishing emotionally or sexually. Her husband might have been distant, disengaged, or just plain uninterested in creating a fulfilling connection. But the Bible is explicit about the fact that husbands and wives are called to mutual care and affection. Paul didn't mince words when he wrote that a husband owes his wife affection (1 Corinthians 7:3). And let's not miss Song of Solomon, where the celebration of desire and intimacy between a husband and wife is on full display.

Too often, society frames intimacy as something women are "obligated" to provide while their needs are overlooked. That's not biblical. Intimacy is meant to be mutual—a sacred exchange of love, affection, and pleasure that strengthens your bond. Potiphar's wife may have been a victim of neglect, but instead of addressing her needs with her husband, she lashed out in a destructive and harmful way. That's the lesson here: ignoring your needs or letting them go unaddressed doesn't make them disappear—it makes them fester.

So what do you do? Have the courage to say, "Babe, this isn't working for me," or, "Here's what I need to feel fulfilled." God didn't design intimacy to be one-sided. It's not just about what he wants; it's about both of you experiencing joy, connection, and pleasure together.

The Gem Being Dropped:

Don't let society or silence chain you. Advocate for your pleasure, honor your needs, and expect your husband to show up in every way. Intimacy is a two-way street; God designed it to strengthen, not stifle, your connection. You deserve to feel loved, seen, and satisfied—mind, body, and soul.

AVOID FALSE RAPE ACCUSATIONS

"...she called to the men of her house and spoke to them, saying, 'See, he has brought in to us a Hebrew to mock us. He came in to me to lie with me, and I cried out with a loud voice. And it happened, when he heard that I lifted my voice and cried out, that he left his garment with me and fled and went outside." (Genesis 39:14-15)

"Therefore, putting away lying, 'Let each one of you speak truth with his neighbor,' for we are members of one another." (Ephesians 4:25)

Scholars often emphasize Potiphar's wife's isolation and the power dynamics in her relationship with Joseph. Her character embodies issues of status, authority, and the constraints faced by women in ancient Egyptian elite households. Carol Meyers, for example, notes that elite women like Potiphar's wife were often socially isolated and restricted in their mobility, leading to situations where longing for companionship or acknowledgment could manifest in complex and sometimes morally ambiguous actions. (Meyers, Women in

Scripture, 2000). With this in mind, I will approach this point from a compassionate and cautionary angle.

First, let's take a compassionate approach. This is a sensitive topic, and it's important to acknowledge the power imbalance between Potiphar's wife and Joseph. However, the historical context is crucial as well. Back then, a woman's voice held little weight. Perhaps Potiphar's wife felt unheard or unseen. Did she lie about the encounter out of desperation, fueled by societal pressures and a lack of agency? Was that her way of asserting dominance and attention? Her false accusation may not be as cut and dry as we think. Despite the complexity of her period for women, still, this story, I believe, provides a healthy background to caution women to never use false rape accusations. Ever. Stats show that it doesn't happen very often, contrary to what society will attempt to paint so that we don't quickly believe when a woman declares she has been raped. Studies indicate that the percentage of false rape accusations is generally low, ranging from around 2% to 10%. It's important to note that the vast majority of sexual assault cases are not fabricated. The perception of false accusations can come from confirmation bias: People may be more likely to remember instances of false accusations, leading to an overestimation of their frequency. And then there's also a misinterpretation of the term "unfounded." Sometimes, cases are deemed "unfounded" due to lack of evidence, not necessarily because the assault didn't occur. This can be misinterpreted as proof of a false accusation. Sister Potiphar is a sobering reminder that it happens every now and then, and when it does, it's not okay to trap men in falsehoods. When the Bible speaks about doing unto others as you would have them do unto to you, it applies in this context. Because no one wants to be lied to.

The Gem Being Dropped:

As far as possible, treat men as you would want. A false accusation doesn't just destroy the accused—it erodes trust, damages credibility, and overshadows the voices of those who desperately need to be heard.

"It's important to note that the vast majority of sexual assault cases are not fabricated."

5

DO NOT USE MEN FOR SEX

"But it happened about this time, when Joseph went into the house to do his work, and none of the men of the house was inside, that she caught him by his garment, saying, 'Lie with me.' But he left his garment in her hand, and fled and ran outside." (Genesis 39:11-12)

"Love suffers long and is kind; love does not envy; love does not parade itself, is not puffed up; does not behave rudely, does not seek its own, is not provoked, thinks no evil." (1 Corinthians 13:4-5)

"Let nothing be done through selfish ambition or conceit, but in lowliness of mind let each esteem others better than himself." (Philippians 2:3)

This principle is timeless: relationships built solely on physical attraction are shaky foundations. True intimacy involves emotional connection, shared values, and mutual respect. Potiphar's wife might have been drawn to Joseph's appearance, but her actions stemmed from a deeper yearning for connection—perhaps a yearning her marriage couldn't fulfill. Men are not to be objectified and seen merely as incubators for our needs and desires. They are human beings who also wish to be loved, cherished, and adored.

Likewise, women are not exempt from the responsibility of rape or assaulting men. The grooming, assault, and sexual objectification of men need to be discussed more openly. Often, it's swept under the rug because men feel ashamed and prefer to talk about it in terms of conquests or rites of passage. But when consent is not given or when there is a significant imbalance of power—such as a much older woman—it's not acceptable to use men in sexually inappropriate ways. The sexual undertones in Potiphar's wife's interactions with Joseph may also reflect underlying power imbalances. As Sidnie White Crawford observes, Potiphar's wife represents "a complex mix of desire, privilege, and frustration," highlighting the limitations placed on women even when they hold certain societal privileges (Eerdmans Dictionary of the Bible, 2000). The story of Potiphar's wife is sometimes interpreted as a cautionary tale about unbridled desire and its consequences. Feminist scholar Phyllis Trible notes that narratives like this one are often built to showcase "the seductive dangers of women who wield sexuality unchecked by moral restraint" (Texts of Terror, 1984). This could imply that her interactions with Joseph explore not only moral failings but also the consequences of exploiting one's power over others in vulnerable positions.

The Gem Being Dropped:

Women are also encouraged to always gain consent from their partners. It's a two-way street. Don't settle for temporary thrills; seek a love that nourishes your soul and makes you feel cherished.

TIME TO DROP YOUR OWN GEMS:

♦ Where have you felt nameless or unseen, known only by others (e.g., someone's wife, daughter, or mother)? How has this impacted your sense of identity?

♦ How have you navigated feelings of loneliness, especially when it comes to unmet desires—emotional, physical, or spiritual? How have these feelings shaped your choices?

♦ Reflect on times when you may have hidden your needs or desires due to shame or societal expectations. What would it mean for you to express these in healthy, God-honoring ways?

♦ Have there been moments where power dynamics in your relationships have influenced your behavior, whether as the one in power or under it? How can you use your influence to build others up rather than exploit or diminish them?

♦ Consider your approach to intimacy in marriage or relationships. How comfortable are you expressing your needs to your partner? What might God be prompting you to do to cultivate a healthier, more open dialogue about intimacy?

- Have you ever felt tempted to sacrifice your values for temporary fulfillment, particularly in moments of vulnerability? How can you build safeguards around your heart and mind to prevent future compromises?

- Reflect on the concept of mutual respect in relationships. How do you ensure that your actions and intentions align with treating others as image-bearers of God rather than as a means to fulfill your unmet needs?

8

LESSONS
FROM
RAHAB

Location: Rahab lived in the city of Jericho, part of the land of Canaan, just before the Israelites conquered it. (Joshua 2:1)

RELATIONSHIP STATUS: MARRIED & REDEEMED.

FAST FACTS:

- Rahab's house was built into the city wall of Jericho, giving her a prime location for hiding the Israelite spies (Joshua 2:15).
- She hid the two spies sent by Joshua and lied to the king's men to protect them (Joshua 2:4-6).
- Rahab is mentioned in Jesus' genealogy and is honored for her faith in the New Testament (Matthew 1:5; Hebrews 11:31; James 2:25).

LIFE EVENTS:

- Rahab harbored the Israelite spies in her home and helped them escape by lowering them out of her window (Joshua 2:15).

- She negotiated with the spies for the safety of her family, and they promised that her household would be spared when Jericho fell (Joshua 2:12-14).

- When the Israelites took Jericho, Rahab and her family were the only ones spared, and she became integrated into the Israelite community (Joshua 6:22-25).

- Rahab married Salmon, and they had a son named Boaz, who would marry Ruth, making Rahab an important part of the lineage of David and Jesus (Matthew 1:5).

THE WOMEN WHO CAN RELATE:

- Women who have had a shameful past or have been labeled by society based on their past choices or lifestyle.

- Women who have engaged in sex work.

- Women who have made bold, faith-driven decisions that set their lives on a different course.

- Women who have been redeemed by God's grace despite a complex or controversial past.

- Women who've used their courage and cunning to protect their families in dangerous situations.

♦ Women who became part of something greater, even after being considered an outsider or an unlikely candidate for greatness.

When you think "love, sex, and relationships," does Rahab's name come to mind? Probably not—but her story will challenge everything you thought you knew. Often dismissed as merely a "prostitute," Rahab's life holds far more than society's labels would suggest.

What if a woman with a past the culture frowns upon could be the one God uses to save a nation? In ancient Jericho, a walled city where women had little agency, Rahab's boldness set her apart. When two Israelite spies showed up at her doorstep, she seized the moment, risking everything to protect them. It's an act of courage that would rewrite her life. She defied expectations, owned her story, and found redemption. Let's dive into what this bold woman can teach us about compassion, worth, and God's unconditional love— no matter where we come from. Rahab's got a story to tell that'll have you dropping major gems all over your girlfriends.

1

CHOOSE COMPASSION OVER JUDGMENT

> *"Then the woman took the two men and hid them; so she said, 'Yes, the men came to me, but I did not know where they were from. And it happened as the gate was being shut, when it was dark, that the men went out." (Joshua 2:4-6)*

> *"He who is without sin among you, let him throw a stone at her first." (John 8:7)*

Globally, there are an estimated 40 to 42 million sex workers, with 80% being women, and nearly three-quarters entering the field due to economic necessity (Business Insider, 2012). In the U.S., around 1 million people are involved in sex work (Public Health Post, 2021). Many face limited choices due to financial pressures, while others, about 5-10%, report pursuing sex work out of personal preference (MCASA, 2022). Violence, legal risks, and limited healthcare access are widespread issues, with up to 45% reporting experiences of physical violence on the job (MCASA, 2022).

With these stats in mind, let's ditch the judgment on women who choose sex work. Many of us haven't walked a mile in the shoes of women who choose sex work. I want us to hold more space for our sisters in this line of work. The sin was not so much the act itself. It's the world that offered a woman with no coin, no family, no hope, nothing but the value of her body. In many instances, women are doing what they can to survive and make it in this world. Rahab's story unfolds in a society where options for women are scarce. The power dynamics were stacked against her. We don't know her whole story, but it's likely she faced poverty, limited choices, or even coercion. Think about it: how many times have we, as women, felt pressured into situations that weren't ideal?

Additionally, yes, there are women who chose this path out of desperation, and there are women who chose this path out of agency. Just like men and women decide to beat up their bodies for sports, beat up their bodies from footballs and basketballs, there are women who choose to make money off of their bodies, too. We don't have to agree, but we do need to withhold judgment. They choose to navigate the world by making a life for themselves in their own way. We must hold space for the modern-day Rahabs because even in the margins, even behind closed doors, even at her place of work, she possessed courage, compassion, and a cunning mind that cannot be ignored. Sex workers are intelligent, hard workers. And deserving of our love and compassion, not stares of judgment and condemnation. Judge them not, for you do not know their stories. Do not paint them all with the same brush. Some are mothers, daughters, and sisters forced into this life by circumstance. Others are survivors, taking control of their destinies. Let us instead advocate for their safety. Let them work openly, without fear of violence or arrest. Let them have access to healthcare, to a roof over their heads. Let them be women, not pariahs.

The Gem Being Dropped:

Sisterhood is vital. Instead of judging, let's practice compassion. The woman next to you may be struggling in a similar way. Offer a listening ear, a non-judgmental space, and a reminder that God's love extends to all of us, no matter our past.

"WE MUST HOLD SPACE FOR THE MODERN-DAY RAHABS OF TODAY."

2

CELEBRATING AGENCY: OWNING YOUR STORY

"Now therefore, I beg you, swear to me by the Lord, since I have shown you kindness, that you also will show kindness to my father's house, and give me a true token, and spare my father, my mother, my brothers, my sisters, and all that they have, and deliver our lives from death." (Joshua 2:12-13)

"Strength and honor are her clothing; she shall rejoice in time to come." (Proverbs 31:2)

Rahab wasn't just a passive victim. She wielded her agency. Just like athletes train their bodies for competition, Rahab used her skills to survive in a harsh environment. She was resourceful, intelligent, and brave. She was a homeowner and had her own business. In a system where women didn't have many viable options to earn a living, she was earning hers the best way she could. However, she got her start, and Rahab is now at the top of her game. Rahab's independence challenges our views on self- sufficiency and societal roles. She used her situation to build a life that reflects her values and strengths. Rahab is giving you permission to own your story. Own your autonomy and ability to make decisions. You don't have to be a damsel in distress.

You always have options. Even if it will take time, energy, and resources. You, woman of God, are powerful, resourceful, and capable of doing the impossible. Just ask Rahab.

And I love Rahab because, like most sex workers, she understands better than the undercover brothers that all the saints are sinners, and God welcomes us with our skeletons and scandals. Of all the places, the men chose her place to spy on Jericho, but she didn't turn them away. She didn't report them. Remember, she's a Canaanite. But she protects them. Rahab, a marginalized woman, takes decisive action to protect the Israelite spies, demonstrating agency in a patriarchal society.

Her courage to defy her city's norms mirrors the courage needed to defy modern societal norms around women's roles.

"YOU ALWAYS HAVE OPTIONS!"

The Gem Being Dropped:

You, too, have agency. Own your story. You can be faithful and flawed. Recognize the strengths and skills you've developed, even if the path wasn't always easy. God can use those experiences to empower you and bless others.

3

YOU ARE A QUEEN DELIVERING YOUR FAMILY

> *"Now the city shall be doomed by the Lord to destruction, it and all who are in it. Only Rahab the harlot shall live, she and all who are with her in the house, because she hid the messengers that we sent." (Joshua 6:17)*

> *"Salmon begot Boaz by Rahab, Boaz begot Obed by Ruth, Obed begot Jesse." (Matthew 1:5)*

Now, here's the real crown jewel of Rahab's story: her worth. Nowhere in scripture does God define her by her profession. He sees her courage, her faith, and her willingness to take a risk. He sees a woman worthy of protection and redemption. She spoke up to the spies (men) and demanded protection and the deliverance of her family. She has a family that she is going to save using her house of prostitution because God can take that thing in your past or even in your present that stains your name with shame and transform it into your deliverance and bring somebody else out with you. I don't know if her roof was their roof or if her food was their food, but when her family's lives were in danger, Rahab saved them. She became the savior of her people, Jericho's Harriet Tubman. Think about what it would take to make such a bold move. She risked everything—her safety, her reputation, her livelihood. Yet, her faith outweighed her fear.

This hits home for me because I've been called names for standing up for women and calling out oppression cloaked in theology. I've been called a Jezebel, a whore, and a disgrace to pastoral ministry. It stung deeply, but like Rahab, I had to dig deep into the well of my soul and remind myself who I am in God's eyes. Those names do not define me, just like they didn't define Rahab. God saw beyond the labels and saw her heart, her strength, and her potential.

Women today still face these same dismissive labels when they dare to stand up for themselves and others. Maybe you're a woman who's been called "difficult" for refusing to stay silent in boardrooms, or "too much" for embracing your femininity and leadership in spaces that try to limit you. Like Rahab, you have to remember that you're not defined by their words. God's definition of you is rooted in your courage, your faith, and your willingness to rise, even when the world tries to pin you down.

Is somebody calling you out of your name today? Don't let anybody, prophet or pastor, define you by what you have done, even if you're still doing it. You are God's child. Women are more than a collection of body parts some want to reduce us to. You have the power to deliver others.

The Gem Being Dropped:

Your worth is not defined by your job, your past, or your mistakes. You are a daughter of God, created in his image. Own your inherent value, and let his love be the foundation of your self-worth.

YOU CAN BE IMPERFECT AND CHOSEN.

"By faith the harlot Rahab did not perish with those who did not believe, when she had received the spies with peace." (Hebrews 11:31) (NKJV)

"Likewise, was not Rahab the harlot also justified by works when she received the messengers and sent them out another way?" (James 2:25)

Rahab wasn't perfect, but God used her anyway. This is a beautiful reminder that God's plans are bigger than our limitations. He works through the messy, the broken, and the unexpected. Dr. Wil Gafney explains, "Rahab was everything that Israel hated and feared: a woman, a sexually active woman controlling her own sexuality, and a Canaanite woman to boot" (Gafney, 2014).

Think about that for a second. Rahab didn't just tick one box on the "unacceptable" list. She embodied multiple identities that made her the epitome of what people in her society condemned. Yet, her faith shone brighter than her circumstances. When I think of

Rahab, I picture a woman standing tall in the midst of a culture that tried to erase her humanity. She was a survivor. She wasn't defined by the labels others gave her. She was bold enough to recognize the God of Israel, even though she wasn't raised to worship Him. That's courage. That's faith.

Let's make it personal. How often do we let our mistakes, our background, or the opinions of others make us feel disqualified from God's promises? Maybe you've been told you're "too much" or "not enough." Maybe the world has slapped labels on you that make you feel like you're on the outside looking in. But just like Rahab, you don't have to fit anyone else's mold to be a part of God's story.

But even though people counted her out, Gafney encourages us, "Don't count a sister out who fears God no matter how the deck is stacked against her. Because Rahab knew God, her circumstances were about to change. And God was going to use the very thing that folk would shame her for to transform her life" (Gafney, 2014).

This makes me think of how God flips the script in our lives. It's like a plot twist in a movie you didn't see coming. God isn't limited by what society says about us. Instead, He rewrites our story. That's what He did for Rahab, and that's what He does for us. Her actions spoke louder than her profession. Her faith overrode her flaws. And as followers of Yahweh, we are called to see people the way God does—through the lens of their faith and not their failures.

Let me share a story. I once met a woman who felt so ashamed of her past that she avoided church altogether. She thought her story would make people judge her, but when she finally opened up, her testimony brought healing to others. Her scars became her testimony. That's Rahab's story too. Her profession doesn't overshadow her faith and role in God's plan, as seen in her pivotal actions.

"I'm so glad Rahab is in Jesus's family tree" (Gafney, 2014). The gospel of Jesus Christ reflected in the life of Rahab is that no matter who you are, no matter what you've done, no matter what has been done to you, nothing can keep you from the safety and salvation of God. Gafney affirms, "Judgemental people may not want you at the table but God says pull up a seat and sit down. Jesus is not ashamed to have you in the family. They may still call you out of your name, but you've got a place in the household of faith, and nobody can put you out. They may still talk about what you used to do, but you're in the Promised Land with them" (Gafney, 2014).

When God calls you, He doesn't ask for your résumé. He's not concerned about your qualifications, but about your willingness to trust Him. Rahab had every reason to believe she'd never amount to anything in God's plan, but her faith rewrote her legacy. Salvation came to Rahab's house. Rahab delivered salvation to her own house. God met her right where she was, bringing her out of her old home to a new life.

Imagine the courage it took for her to hang that scarlet cord out of her window. She risked everything on a God she barely knew. That scarlet cord wasn't just a signal—it was a statement of faith. What's your scarlet cord? What's the step of faith you need to take, even when it doesn't make sense? Rahab's inclusion in the genealogy of Jesus in Matthew highlights her significance despite her background as a Canaanite sex worker. This intersectionality underlines the importance of embracing all aspects of one's identity. Rahab's story shows that faith is a journey, and God can work through us regardless of our past. Her story exemplifies grace and transformation, aligning perfectly with the message of the Gospel.

"WHEN GOD CALLS YOU, HE DOESN'T ASK FOR YOUR RÉSUMÉ"

The Gem Being Dropped:

Your past doesn't disqualify you—it positions you. The very thing people shame you for is what God can use to transform your life and others. You don't have to be perfect to be chosen. God specializes in using the unexpected, the overlooked, and the imperfect to fulfill His perfect plan. So, pull up your seat at the table—God reserved it just for you.[1]

Wil Gafney, "Who Are You Calling A Whore?," Womanists Wading in the Word™, October 19, 2014, https://www.wilgafney.com/2014/10/19/who-are-you-calling-a-whore/.

TIME TO DROP YOUR OWN GEMS:

♦ How do societal expectations sometimes limit your choices or push you into situations you might not have chosen freely?

♦ Think of a time when you felt pressured into survival choices or situations that others may not understand. How can you begin to show compassion for yourself and let go of the shame attached to those experiences?

♦ Where do you need to exercise agency in your life today, owning your story and using your unique strengths, just as Rahab did? What steps can you take to honor your power, even if it feels uncomfortable?

♦ Have you ever felt judged for your past or present circumstances? How can we, as Christian women, cultivate a more compassionate and understanding community?

♦ What does "worth" mean to you? How can you connect with your inherent value as a woman of God, regardless of your profession or background?

◆ Can you think of a time when God used an unexpected person or situation to work in your life? Share your story!

◆ How does Rahab's inclusion in the lineage of Jesus invite you to embrace the fullness of your identity?

◆ Rahab's story shows that faith and courage often go hand in hand. What bold steps of faith is God calling you to take, even if they challenge societal expectations or feel risky? How can you lean into this courage today?

_____

_____

_____

_____

_____

_____

_____

_____

_____

_____

_____

_____

9

LESSONS FROM RUTH & NAOMI

Location: Moab and then later Bethlehem, in the land of Judah (Ruth 1:1, Ruth 1:6,7, Ruth 1:22)

RELATIONSHIP STATUS: REMARRIED & WIDOWED

FAST FACTS:

- Ruth was a Moabite, meaning she came from a foreign land, and people were often seen as outsiders by Israelites (Ruth 1:4).
- Naomi, marked by her sorrow, renamed herself "Mara" (meaning "bitter") to express her grief and sense of loss (Ruth 1:20).
- Ruth's declaration of loyalty to Naomi—"Where you go, I will go..." (Ruth 1:16)—is one of the most famous lines in Scripture, symbolizing her steadfastness and love.
- Ruth became the great-grandmother of King David (Ruth 4:17) and, thus, part of the lineage of Jesus (Matthew 1:5-6).

LIFE EVENTS:

- After her husband and sons died, Naomi decided to return to Bethlehem and Ruth chose to go with her, leaving her homeland behind (Ruth 1:16-18).
- Ruth gleaned in the fields of Boaz, a relative of Naomi, to provide for herself and Naomi (Ruth 2:2-3).
- Boaz showed kindness to Ruth, offering her protection and food, eventually agreeing to redeem her by marrying her and securing her and Naomi's future (Ruth 4:1-10).
- Ruth gave birth to a son, Obed, who would become the grandfather of King David (Ruth 4:13-17).

THE WOMEN WHO CAN RELATE:

- Widows or women who've had to start over after loss, rebuilding their lives from scratch with resilience and faith.
- Women who share deep, supportive bonds with their mothers-in-law or chosen family, navigating complex family dynamics with love.
- Women known for their fierce loyalty and dedication, staying committed even through hardship.
- Outsiders who've found a way to belong and create impact in unfamiliar or unwelcoming spaces.
- Single women who bear the weight of societal judgment or add-

ed responsibilities but continue to press forward.

- ◆ Hardworking women who take on multiple roles to support themselves and those they care for.
- ◆ Women who've felt the power of redemption through faith, relationships, or fresh beginnings, transforming their stories into testimonies.
- ◆ Women who have married older men or found stability in unexpected relationships

If I hear one more person tell somebody to be like Ruth and wait on your Boaz, I will scream. The way Ruth has been typecast into every single woman of faith's dream is nauseating. Okay, maybe not nauseating, but her story is worthy of much more study and introspection. She can't be reduced to her value and worth being measured by a man finding her and caring for her. There's so much more to the story, for sure. Many paint Ruth and Naomi with a single brushstroke: the loyal daughter-in-law and the bitter widow. But beneath the surface lies a symphony of resilience, fierce love, and courage that challenges societal norms. Their story isn't just about purity; it's about sex, desire, and the complex dance of navigating intimacy in a world far removed from our own. We also know that God is working in this story. We see Yahweh's fingerprints throughout it. God's involvement in this story is not a footnote; it's a fact. Still, I want to locate some gems between the lines of God's providence. I want us to be geologists who go beneath the surface and see what Ruth has to say to us, especially against the backdrop of God always coming through for His daughters.

YOU ARE NOT A MONOLITH. YOU HAVE YOUR OWN IDENTITY.

> *"But Ruth said: 'Entreat me not to leave you, or to turn back from following after you; for wherever you go, I will go; and wherever you lodge, I will lodge; your people shall be my people, and your God, my God.'" (Ruth 1:16)*

> *"There is neither Jew nor Greek, there is neither slave nor free, there is neither male nor female; for you are all one in Christ Jesus." (Galatians 3:28)*

Ruth was a Moabite. She was not an Israelite. Moabites were known to come from a lineage of incest. Women were believed to be temptresses and seductresses, pagans, and enemies of Israel. Through incestuous relations, the Moabites were descendants of Lot, Abraham's nephew (Genesis 19). This, along with historical conflicts, led to a generally negative view of Moabites among the Israelites. Moabite women, in particular, carried the stigma of being temptresses, a stereotype deeply rooted in the story of Balak's attempt to curse Israel through the prophet Balaam (Numbers 22-24). This is important to highlight because many women come from less-than-stellar backgrounds.

We have women in our families who were labeled as homewreckers, gold diggers, unfit mothers, demanding, and overbearing. Ruth teaches us that just because you come from a family, community, neighborhood, or ethnicity where women are painted with a particular stereotype, it does not mean, by any stretch of the imagination, that you have to identify with that stereotype. Just because people say all Black women are strong, loud, welfare queens, or jezebels with a dash of mammy qualities does not mean you must align with that identity. You are your own person. You are your own identity, with unique qualities and quirks that only you possess. Don't give in to the pressure and history of stereotypes that don't apply to you. Just because Ruth was a Moabite doesn't mean she acted like one or aligned her actions with traditional Moabite views and beliefs. You can be different. You can be someone who defies and challenges stereotypes by being your own person. You are a daughter, a sister, a wife, a worker, and a woman of faith. Your identity is profound and multi-faceted. Don't let anyone reduce you to a single label.

"THE ONLY LABELS YOU NEED TO WEAR ARE THE ONES ON YOUR CLOTHES!"

The Gem Being Dropped:

The only labels you need to wear are the ones on your clothes. Don't ever feel like you have to accept the labels people place on you simply because you exist or because of who your family is. Your life has always been a counternarrative to stereotypes.

2

YOU CAN SURVIVE WHAT
YOU DIDN'T CHOOSE.

"Then Elimelech, Naomi's husband, died; and she was left, and her two sons. Now they took wives of the women of Moab: the name of the one was Orpah, and the name of the other Ruth. And they dwelt there about ten years. Then both Mahlon and Chilion also died; so the woman survived her two sons and her husband." (Ruth 1:3-5)

"When you pass through the waters, I will be with you; and through the rivers, they shall not overflow you. When you walk through the fire, you shall not be burned, nor shall the flame scorch you." (Isaiah 43:2)

Ruth's journey into Ephrathite society was undoubtedly fraught with challenges. Traditionally, we teach that Ruth married into the Bethlehemite family willingly, or we assume that she wanted to marry into this family. This traditional reading of the text happens when we ignore voices that are not being heard in the text—specifically, the voices of women who are significant characters in the story. In her book, Womanist Midrash, Dr. Wilda Gafney suggests a closer reading of the text reveals that the Hebrew word for marriage used in Ruth 1 suggests a strong element of being forced into this marriage. The Hebrew word ns has strong overtones of one being seized or carried into. The verb used in this text is generally employed in two ways. The verb often carries the connotation of taking something by force, as in the case of war or plunder. For example, men take women as spoils of war. The second way the verb is often used in Scripture is for taking possession of something, such as land or property. Some scholars say that the men taking Ruth and Orpah as wives is a neutral statement. And while ns can be used in contexts involving the possession of something, its use in direct relation to marriage is not as prevalent in Scripture.

This observation supports the argument that ns in Ruth 1:4 might carry a more forceful or negative connotation than a simple act of taking a wife.

Let me explain further. Imagine a big, pink toy box filled with many pretty dolls and sparkly dresses. There are lots of dolls to play with. Now, imagine you're looking for a doll that wears a crown. You might find a few dolls with crowns, but not as many as dolls without crowns. Just like there are more dolls without crowns, there are more words for "getting married" than words with crowns that mean "taking someone forcefully." So, when we find a doll with a crown suggesting "taking someone forcefully," it's special because it's not what we usually see in Scripture. It makes us think, "Hmm, this word is different. Maybe it means something important." We should pay attention to it and consider what it could mean. The question then becomes: Why did the writer choose that term instead of a more positive, loving term when describing the marriage that took place? Why not the typical words used around marriage in Scripture? The Hebrew word ns (to lift or carry) to describe the marriage of Ruth's relatives suggests a potential power imbalance and the possibility of coercion. Take all the time you need to sit with that statement.

From Ruth's perspective, this raises questions about the agency she had in these marriages. Did she have a genuine choice in the matter? We can't say for sure. Here's what Ruth could say to us, though: You can survive what you didn't choose. You can survive the challenges, obstacles, and struggles that come from being thrust into situations you didn't choose for yourself. You will not die from it. You will come out of it better than how you came in. Things will get better. You will find yourself again, and even though you didn't choose the situation, you will have the power and strength to survive beyond what chooses you.

The Gem Being Dropped:

You didn't choose your family. You didn't choose that negative, traumatic experience. You didn't choose to be cheated on. You didn't choose to experience the loss of loved ones. You didn't choose the horrible things done to you. But I promise you will survive what you didn't choose.

"YOU CAN SURVIVE THE CHALLENGES, OBSTACLES, AND STRUGGLES THAT COME FROM BEING THRUST INTO SITUATIONS YOU DIDN'T CHOOSE FOR YOUR-SELF."

3

YOU'RE NOT WRONG FOR STAYING OR FOR LEAVING. BEING SUPPORTED IS KEY.

"And Naomi said to her two daughters-in-law, 'Go, return each to her mother's house. The Lord deal kindly with you, as you have dealt with the dead and with me. The Lord grant that you may find rest, each in the house of her husband.'" (Ruth 1:8-9)

"Two are better than one, because they have a good reward for their labor. For if they fall, one will lift up his companion. But woe to him who is alone when he falls, for he has no one to help him up." (Ecclesiastes 4:9-10)

Following the train of thought that it's likely Ruth was coerced into Naomi's family, everything shifts around the narrative we've been traditionally spoon-fed all these years. I see now why Naomi was like, "You can return to your mommy, daughter. I'm no good for you, and apparently, you're no good for me either, given your non-Israelite background, your non-Israelite lineage, and how you even possibly ended up in my family." Naomi was telling her to go back to her gods, go back to her people, and go back to your foreign and wrong ways. And yet, Ruth stayed with her. And I understand why. Whew, I understand. I mean, it's no wonder she chose to follow the God of Naomi. She was in a desperate situation. There must've been pressure to survive and thrive in a society that left her vulnerable and alone. It's giving, "I'll resign to the reality of my condition and make decisions to survive my condition." So if that means sticking with the forced mother-in-law I didn't choose, I'll do it. I'm down if that means following her beliefs, customs, and habits. Because at least I'll have a support system. At least I'll have some form of shelter. At least I'll have companionship. At least I'll have somebody.

Despite the details surrounding the narrative, Ruth and Naomi seemingly forge a friendship. Naomi blesses her in Ruth 1: 8,9. From this narrative, we see that they support one another. Two women from diverse backgrounds AND different generations. She's young in the prime of life, and the other, old beyond childbearing years, illustrates they were able to make it work. There was a relationship there.

There was support there. And so Ruth would tell us that when you are in the midst of a difficult situation, when you are in new territory, a new city, a new job, a relationship, a new mindset, secure the support you need to thrive the best way you know how.

Orpah wasn't wrong for leaving. Ruth wasn't wrong for staying. Orpah chose to find support back in Moab. Ruth chose her support system by staying with Naomi. Both are valid. You get to choose yours as well. There are so many women who made the difficult choice to stay. Stay in broken homes, demanding jobs, and problematic relationships. They stayed in foreign, uncomfortable societies and experiences if it meant their survival and helping the next generation. They stayed as enslaved people instead of escaping like Harriet Tubman. They stayed when they could've gone somewhere else. Both versions of survival and support are valid. Ruth celebrates and acknowledges women who choose to find their support by staying.

The Gem Being Dropped:

Hold space for women who choose to stay. Don't judge or condemn; instead, listen to their stories with compassion and grace.

GO AHEAD AND UNCOVER HIS HARDWORKING, DUSTY FEET, SIS.

> *"And after Boaz had eaten and drunk, and his heart was cheerful, he went to lie down at the end of the heap of grain; and she came softly, uncovered his feet, and lay down. Now it happened at midnight that the man was startled, and turned himself; and there, a woman was lying at his feet. And he said, 'Who are you?' So she answered, 'I am Ruth, your maidservant. Take your maidservant under your wing, for you are a close relative.'"*
> *(Ruth 3:7-9)*

> *"And my God shall supply all your need according to His riches in glory by Christ Jesus."(Philippians 4:19)*

Understand that life insurance policies and retirement plans didn't exist in Ruth's times, and so many widows had to do what was necessary to find protection, work, and sometimes even food. Thanks be to God for providing a way for women to be cared for. God instituted the law of the family redeemer in Deuteronomy 25, which states that a deceased man's brother would marry and care for his brother's widow. And any man who refused to take care of his brother's widow was considered an embarrassment and disgrace. All this was intended to provide for Israelite widows. But remember, Ruth was a Moabite. Still, according to this law, Boaz steps in and redeems Ruth and marries her.

What makes this story so powerful for women, though, is not so much that Boaz marries Ruth. It's the agency and autonomy that Ruth employs to take control of her destiny. Ruth reminds us that we are worthy of being protected and provided for. We are worthy of being loved, adored, and cherished, regardless of our Moabite tendencies or affiliations. We. Are. Worthy.

In Chapter 2, Ruth initially feels like she is just a foreigner. Just an outcast. Just an outsider. Just another woman who didn't fit into the typical boxes of women who should be cared for and loved. Maybe you feel like you're just a foreigner. You're just a single mom. You're just in your 40s. You're just a professional black woman and intimidating to men. You're just a woman that's not a virgin. You're just a woman who's not as respectable, well-spoken, and educated. You're just a woman who's too big, too small, too loud, too quiet, too much, not enough, and on and on. Oh, but the Ruth of chapter 3 goes through a shift. She changes out of her work clothes and foreign clothes, bathes, puts on some perfumes and finds herself intentionally in Boaz's space.

Traditionally, we like to sexualize this moment. We want to make it feel more romantic and sexy. Rather than a sexually suggestive act, the uncovering of Boaz's feet was a culturally and legally significant gesture within the context of ancient Israelite society. It represented a public declaration of Ruth's desire for a kinsman-redeemer to fulfill his obligations under the laws of levirate marriage and redemption. She was letting everybody know, particularly Boaz, that she was worthy and deserving of being taken care of, provided for, and honored. She was making a serious and formal proposal to have her needs met for the rest of her life. She was being proactive.

Sis. We must embody Ruth's boldness to honor her desire to be covered and cared for. I need us to release the trauma and brokenness around feeling like we have to suffer through life alone and do everything by ourselves. That is not your birthright. You are deserving of SUPPORT. And I will take it a step further and declare that you, daughter of God, deserve support from good brothers who will protect, provide, and pursue you if that's what you truly want. Do not settle for anything less. Make your request known and watch God work on your behalf.

"You are deserving of SUPPORT."

The Gem Being Dropped:

You better look for men with good feet to uncover! Position yourself to find men who have the means, desire, and capacity to make life easier and lighter for you. Don't for a minute give in to the false belief that your past, background, or even current circumstance precludes you from having a Boaz in your life. Bonus: also, positioning is not the same as begging. She let Boaz know one time, and then it was up to him to make moves.

5

TELL YOUR OWN STORY, SIS.

"Then the women said to Naomi, 'Blessed be the Lord, who has not left you this day without a close relative; and may his name be famous in Israel! And may he be to you a restorer of life and a nourisher of your old age; for your daughter-in-law, who loves you, who is better to you than seven sons, has borne him.'" (Ruth 4:14-15)

"Let the redeemed of the Lord say so, whom He has redeemed from the hand of the enemy." (Psalm 107:2)

"'Return to your own house, and tell what great things God has done for you.' And he went his way and proclaimed throughout the whole city what great things Jesus had done for him." (Luke 8:39)

Here's the reality. The book of Ruth would've been different if Ruth had written it herself. Period. Ruth, writing this book from the perspective of a foreign migrant woman who had to survive and be resilient, would've used a different tone. Let's be clear. The purpose of the book is masculine. The book of Ruth is in the Bible to chronicle David's genealogy. That doesn't make it wrong. It's just the truth.

In this story, Ruth's being a Moabite amplifies her impact and necessity only because it bolsters the Hebrew national identity. As the United Religions Initiative aptly points out "The views and the spirituality in these religions are based on the experiences, problems, questions, feelings, insights, and interests of men and on men's desires, fears, dreams, and fantasies. In the age-old practice of male domination in these world religions, men with such androcentric, patriarchal views consider themselves superior to women. They claim exclusive authority to determine how God must be viewed, what is human, male, and female, and to identify God's allocation of roles and responsibilities among men and women." 1

In most biblical texts, there's an emphasis on masculine interests and what makes a woman worthy based on how it serves the man. For example, in Ruth 3:10, Boaz exclaims that you're showing more loyalty to the family by choosing him and not some younger man. There is nothing about choosing this for herself or her interests but for the family. Even by the end of the story, once she has the coveted baby, Obed, Ruth's name vanishes from the story. The women name the child and identify the baby as Naomi's child, not Ruth's. That's major. Yes, we see her name again in the genealogy of Jesus, but that, to me, as the preachers call it, is an easy shout.

In this chapter, I want to stretch and challenge us as women. I believe Ruth would like us to know that, in many instances, your silence is not your strength. Your voice matters to God, and so your voice should still matter to you. No matter how much society, men, communities, churches, institutions, and politics try to silence and obscure your voice and story? Don't ever forget that your voice is of utmost importance. You are not to be discarded or forgotten like an incubator, reduced to your function and stripped of your identity. The shout is because God remembers you; don't you ever forget you!

The Gem Being Dropped:

Celebrate and acknowledge your version of the story. Celebrate and hold dear your narrative of what happened to you. Don't let others minimize or reduce how you show up. Because if God saw fit to remember Ruth, your story is worth remembering, too.[2]

United Religions Initiative. "Challenging Androcentrism." URI Stories, 24 Feb. 2009, https://www.uri.org/uri-story/20090224-challenging-androcentrism.

6

THERE'S POWER IN THE INTERGENERATIONAL WISDOM OF SISTERS

"But Ruth said: 'Entreat me not to leave you, or to turn back from following after you; for wherever you go, I will go; and wherever you lodge, I will lodge; your people shall be my people, and your God, my God. Where you die, I will die, and there will I be buried. The Lord do so to me, and more also, if anything but death parts you and me.'" (Ruth 1:16-17)

"The older women likewise, that they be reverent in behavior, not slanderers, not given to much wine, teachers of good things – that they admonish the young women to love their husbands, to love their children." (Titus 2:3-4)

There's a secret power in the sisterhood that flows between generations. And when I say power, I mean the kind that can shift your perspective, breathe life into your tired spirit, and even help you find a deeper understanding of God's love. I've felt it firsthand, and I know it to be true because some of the best decisions I've ever made involved linking arms with women who've walked a little further down the road than me.

In my teachings about the S5 lifestyle, sisterhood stands as one of the five pillars, emphasizing that we are better, stronger, and more powerful when we walk together. Sisterhood is a divine design—it reflects God's intention for community, mutual support, and accountability among women. It's about creating spaces where women can be vulnerable without fear of judgment, celebrate each other's victories without comparison, and lean on one another during life's challenges.

I now have a prayer partner who's older than me, and I look forward to her prayers and advice. She carries wisdom that she can't just pick up on social media or read in a book. No, her prayers have a weight and authority that only years of faith and experience can give. I want all women of God to experience this in their lives.

Do you have older women you can talk to about anything? Can younger women come to you and talk about what they're currently facing without judgment?

When I look at Ruth and Naomi, I see much more than a family story. This was a moment of radical choice, of stepping into the unknown together. Naomi, bitter from loss and heartache, tries pushing Ruth away. But Ruth's loyalty runs deep; she doesn't just cling to Naomi; she makes a promise. "Where you go, I will go; your people shall be my people, and your God, my God." (Ruth 1:16) She's not just along for the ride. Ruth chooses to be taught by Naomi's life, experiences, and relationship with God. And in that moment, they both gain something powerful—an unbreakable bond of love, wisdom, and resilience.

This is what intergenerational sisterhood looks like, and in the S5 lifestyle, we recognize this as a God-given reflection of unity and strength. Sisterhood in this context isn't about surface-level connections; it's rooted in love, shared purpose, and a commitment to growth, healing, and empowerment. It celebrates individuality while fostering accountability and safe spaces for healing.

Too often, we overlook the deep well of wisdom our older sisters hold. We assume their experiences are outdated, irrelevant or that their story is written in a language we can't understand. But these women carry keys to the faith that kept them through storms, the love that anchored them, and the hope that helped them believe again. Their scars tell stories and their victories light a path we can walk. My sisterhood has blessed me with women who've walked through fire and come out stronger. And I'm here to tell you: don't miss out on the power of that connection just because it might look different or feel uncomfortable at first.

Often in ministry, I see older women gathering together and younger women sitting on the sidelines, unsure if there's a seat at the table for them. I've been asked so many times how we get younger women to show up and engage. But maybe the question should be, "How do we show them that this space isn't just for the older ladies—it's for all of us?"

Ruth and Naomi's story shows us that sisterhood isn't about age; it's about the courage to lean in, to teach and be taught, to love and be loved, regardless of where we are. It's not just about filling a room; it's about creating meaningful connections. Everyone benefits when younger and older women come together in spaces of mutual respect and openness.

The Gem Being Dropped:

Don't sleep on this kind of sisterhood. When we come together—older and younger—there's something unstoppable that God can do in our lives. So reach out, seek that wisdom, and share your story. You might find that the support you're craving is waiting in the heart of another sister who's been where you're standing. We're stronger, wiser, and braver when we walk this journey together.

7

LIBERATE YOURSELF FROM BEING A PERFECTIONIST AND OVERPERFORMER

"So Ruth the Moabitess said to Naomi, 'Please let me go to the field, and glean heads of grain after him in whose sight I may find favor.' And she said to her, 'Go, my daughter.' Then she left, and went and gleaned in the field after the reapers.

And she happened to come to the part of the field belonging to Boaz, who was of the family of Elimelech." (Ruth 2:2-3)

I'm a recovering perfectionist, a Black woman who has spent much of her life working, preaching, and singing—all to earn validation, acceptance, worthiness, and love. For so long, I believed that the only way to matter was to overperform, be perfect, and meet impossible standards. Ruth's story, though, offers a revolutionary invitation for Black women to step off that treadmill of proving and performing. Ruth's gleaning in Boaz's field challenges the idea that we must earn our right to rest, acceptance, and belonging. Instead, her story whispers a liberating, radical truth: we are enough, just as we are.

In the ancient practice of gleaning, Ruth gathered the overlooked, the left behind, and the "leftovers." But her work wasn't about overachievement or striving for applause. She wasn't in that field to prove her worth or make a name for herself. She gleaned because it was her right, as someone in need, to have a share of the community's resources. Israelite law required farmers to leave some crops for people like Ruth—widows, orphans, and foreigners—so they could sustain themselves with dignity. This wasn't charity; it was a form of justice, a built-in safety net for those who society often marginalized.

For Black women, gleaning can be a metaphor for liberating ourselves from the crushing weight of overperformance and perfectionism. Ruth didn't have to "earn" her right to glean. She didn't have to hustle harder or outshine others to gather what was rightfully hers. Her worth wasn't measured by how many slivers of grain she could collect in a day or how perfectly she could perform. Instead, Ruth teaches us to claim the "enoughness" that is ours by design—an identity that doesn't require proving, performing, or exhausting ourselves to be valuable.

In my life, I've seen how the expectation to "do it all" has often left me feeling depleted, stretched beyond my limits, and convinced that I had to keep showing up perfectly to be worthy. But Ruth's story is a balm for that weary perfectionist spirit. It invites me, and all Black women, to shift from striving to belonging. She reminds us that we are enough, even when we're simply showing up in our fields, doing what we can with what we have. We don't have to be superheroes. We don't have to be flawless. We are worthy of love, respect, and rest, even when we feel like we're just gathering life's leftovers.

Ruth's story tells us we can be vulnerable and imperfect and still be valued. Ruth champions the beauty of simply being in a world that often measures Black women by our productivity and resilience. She teaches us that there's strength in knowing our limits, asking for what we need, and standing up for our right to rest. We are allowed to stop, to say, "This is enough," and to reject any narrative that insists we must do it all to be worthy. We, like Ruth, deserve spaces where our work is honored, our rest is protected, and our humanity is celebrated without conditions.

The Gem Being Dropped:

Embrace your enoughness, sis. Liberate yourself from the lie that you must be perfect or overperform to be worthy. Like Ruth gleaning in the field, you can rest in the truth that you're already enough, even as you gather the blessings left for you. It's time to release the weight of proving and step into the freedom of being.

TIME TO DROP YOUR OWN GEMS:

- What labels or stereotypes have you felt pressured to live up to or unfairly placed on you? How have these labels shaped your sense of identity, and what would it mean to let them go?

- In what areas of your life are you navigating situations you didn't choose? How are you finding resilience, or where do you need more support to survive and thrive in these spaces?

- How do you evaluate your support systems when faced with the decision to stay or leave a challenging situation? Reflect on a time when you either stayed or left; what did it teach you about your boundaries, resilience, and the importance of companionship?

- Consider your desires for protection, provision, and support. What would it mean to confidently pursue these things without diminishing your worth or settling?

- If you could tell your story from your perspective, unfiltered and in your own words, what truths would you include that might typically go unspoken? What parts of your story deserve to be celebrated and acknowledged fully?

♦ Reflect on a piece of wisdom or guidance you've received from another woman that changed your perspective. What intergenerational wisdom have you gained or would like to pass on, especially around relationships, resilience, or faith?

♦ What parts of yourself—talents, needs, imperfections, or dreams—have you felt pressured to hide, perfect, or overextend to feel worthy of love, acceptance, or validation? How would it feel to embrace these parts of yourself as already enough, just as they are?

10

LESSONS
FROM
HANNAH

Location: Hannah lived in Ramah, in the hill country of Ephraim, and frequently traveled to Shiloh, where the Tabernacle of the Lord was located (1 Samuel 1:1, 3).

RELATIONSHIP STATUS: POLYGAMOUS & PRAYING

FAST FACTS:

- Hannah's name means "grace" or "favor," she is known for her faithful prayer and devotion to God.
- She vowed to God that if He gave her a son, she would dedicate him to the Lord's service for life (1 Samuel 1:11).
- After giving birth to Samuel, Hannah composed a song of praise (1 Samuel 2:1-10), often compared to Mary's Magnificat in the New Testament.

LIFE EVENTS:

- Hannah was barren for many years and faced ridicule from Penninah, Elkanah's other wife, for not having children (1 Samuel 1:6-7).
- She went to the tabernacle in Shiloh, where she prayed fervently and vowed to the Lord, asking for a son (1 Samuel 1:9-11).
- God answered her prayer, and she gave birth to Samuel, whom she later dedicated to the Lord as promised (1 Samuel 1:19-28).
- Hannah's faithfulness resulted in having more children after Samuel, as God blessed her with several more sons and daughters (1 Samuel 2:21).

THE WOMEN WHO CAN RELATE:

- Women who've poured out their hearts to God in raw, desperate prayers during life's most challenging moments.
- Women who've faced ridicule or judgment from others regarding deeply personal struggles, especially around fertility or family dynamics.
- Women navigating challenging or competitive family relationships, including polygamous or blended family dynamics.
- Women who've endured well-meaning but misguided comments from loved ones who don't fully understand their pain.
- Women discovering the freedom of vulnerability with God,

shedding the pressure to appear composed or "put-together."

♦ Women who've experienced God's faithfulness and answered prayers after long seasons of waiting and hoping.

♦ Women who've turned their deepest pain into acts of service, using their stories to inspire and uplift others.

You might know her story from that tear-jerking scene where she prays desperately for a child. But Hannah is a whole woman, and her journey in 1 Samuel 1 and 2 is packed with gems for us today. Some folks paint her as the ultimate submissive wife, silently suffering for a son. But we'll see that Hannah fiercely advocates for herself and her desires.

1

TRUST GOD'S TIMING

> *"So it came to pass in the process of time that Hannah conceived and bore a son, and called his name Samuel, saying, 'Because I have asked for him from the Lord.'"*
> *(1 Samuel 1:20)*

> *"Wait on the Lord; be of good courage, and He shall strengthen your heart; wait, I say, on the Lord!" (Psalm 27:14)*

There was a time when I had to wait for my visa to come through. It took several years. During that long season, I couldn't leave the country. I couldn't travel home for the holidays, attend international speaking engagements, or even take vacations on my beloved island of Jamaica. For three long years, I had to stay put. I had to trust the timing of the government to issue my green card so I could become a permanent resident. It was a process that demanded patience, faith, and much waiting.

When it comes to relationships, the waiting can feel just as endless. For those of us who desire marriage, it often feels like forever. I've been single for most of my life with a deep longing for marriage, and there have been many days when I've cried out, "Lord, how much longer? This is taking forever. Where is the man I can build a life with?"

It's even harder when it feels like everyone else is getting what you want. Social media doesn't make it any easier—seeing relationship pics, vacation snapshots, and engagement announcements can make you feel like life is passing you by.

In such moments, I imagine Hannah gently taking our hands, looking us in the eyes, and reminding us that God's timing doesn't always make sense, but it is always perfect.

Hannah waited years for her son, Samuel. When he finally arrived, I believe he was worth every tear, prayer, sleepless night, and moment of doubt.

Hannah would want us to know that God hears our cries, sees our desires, and cares deeply about them because they matter to us. So yes, be encouraged. Hold on tight. Trust that God's promises are worth the wait.

"TRUST THAT GOD'S PROMISES ARE WORTH THE WAIT."

The Gem Being Dropped:

Trusting in God's timing means surrendering your plans to His wisdom, knowing that what He has in store is better than anything you could imagine. Hang tight and lean into the waiting—it's worth it.

UNDERSTAND THAT A PARTNER CAN'T FILL EVERY VOID

"Then Elkanah, her husband, said to her, 'Hannah, why do you weep? Why do you not eat? And why is your heart grieved? Am I not better to you than ten sons?'" (1 Samuel 1:8)

My nephew loves puzzles. He loves to put them together. One day, we were assembling a puzzle and making progress. He was doing most of the work because he's way better at puzzles than I am. Completing the puzzle is like relationships. They require teamwork, patience, support, and encouragement.

On this particular day, we were almost finished but couldn't find the final piece. We searched everywhere—up and down, all over the living room and kitchen—trying to locate this missing puzzle piece. We kept searching because no matter how perfect the rest of the puzzle is, it remains incomplete without that one missing piece. This missing piece represents the internal voids and heartaches that only God can fill and heal.

When you are in a relationship with someone, even with the

most loving and supportive partner like Elkanah was to Hannah, there will be voids that no human can fill. There will be pain and heartache that no man can heal and restore. Just as the puzzle remains incomplete without that missing piece, our lives can feel incomplete if we rely solely on our partners for fulfillment. Your emotional, mental, and spiritual health needs to seek strength and healing from within and from your Creator, who truly understands and can heal the depths of your pain. I remember the scripture, "God heals the brokenhearted and binds up their wounds." (Psalm 147:3)

The Gem Being Dropped:

It's okay to acknowledge that men can't heal every broken part of you. It's okay to live in the reality that sometimes only God understands, and only God, therapy, and prayer can heal specific parts of you.

3

POUR OUT YOUR HEART TO GOD

"And she was in bitterness of soul and prayed to the Lord and wept in anguish. Then she made a vow and said, 'O Lord of hosts, if You will indeed look on the affliction of Your maidservant and remember me...'" (1 Samuel 1:10-11)

"Trust in Him at all times, you people; pour out your heart before Him; God is a refuge for us." (Psalm 62:8)

"Be anxious for nothing, but in everything by prayer and supplication, with thanksgiving, let your requests be made known to God; and the peace of God, which surpasses all understanding, will guard your hearts and minds through Christ Jesus." (Philippians 4:6-7)

My most powerful moments with God have been when I am the most vulnerable and transparent. As a high-achieving, perfectionist, driven, good-girl mentality black woman, even in my relationship with God, it hasn't always been easy to be honest and authentic. Because it's been drilled into me that I'm expected to be a certain way and act a certain way—even with the Lord. There's also a genuine fear that our Creator won't accept or understand me. Hannah is in scripture to permit us to unabashedly pour our hearts into the Lord without holding anything back.

As women, we are taught feminine etiquette at an early age. Keep your legs closed when sitting. Walk a certain way when you're in heels. Don't slouch. Don't laugh too loudly. Don't wear a hair bonnet or pajamas outside. I'm not here to knock or elevate these rules of etiquette. But when pouring out your heart to God, the only rule is not to hold back. Let it all out.

Regarding your relationship with God, it's not the time to be prim and proper. It's not the time to fulfill some unspoken good girl rule book. It's time to pour it out. All the way out.

There are too many physical ailments plaguing black women because we don't have safe spaces to let our emotions out. When Hannah was at her lowest, she went to the sanctuary and poured out her heart to God. To the point that the priest, Eli, thought she was tipsy. It was an ugly cry. It was a "lashes gone" kinda cry. When was the last time you had an ugly cry experience with your Lord? When was the last time you poured out your heart to Him in such a way that there would be nothing left to say? I invite you to embrace your inner Hannah and boldly come to your Heavenly Father, willing to pour your heart out completely to God. God promises to hear us and comfort the vulnerable, honest, authentic version of ourselves, not our representative. To truly thrive in relationships, don't be afraid to push forward, open your heart to God, and allow His love to bring out the best in you.. Don't be scared to get raw and honest with Him. Tell Him your fears, hopes, dreams, and frustrations. He can handle it.

The Gem Being Dropped:

Don't hold back with God. Pour out your heart completely, knowing He values your vulnerable, authentic version. There is power in coming to God without pretenses, letting Him see your true self.

YOU'RE STILL WORTHY
WHEN YOUR BODY SAYS NO

"And her rival also provoked her severely, to make her miserable, because the Lord had closed her womb. So it was, year by year, when she went up to the house of the Lord, that she provoked her; therefore, she wept and did not eat." (1 Samuel 1:6-7)

Infertility can feel like a betrayal—a cruel twist of fate against your deepest desires. For Hannah, the pain was layered. Not only was she unable to conceive, but she was tormented by Peninnah, her rival, who mocked her year after year. It's a pain many women know too well—the sting of wanting something so deeply while being reminded, sometimes cruelly, of what you lack.

Hannah's story doesn't shy away from the messy emotions: the rawness of her weeping, her desperate prayers, and her envy of Peninnah's full womb. But Hannah's inability to conceive didn't define her. She didn't allow her barrenness to strip her of her identity or her faith. Instead, she took her heartbreak to God. She poured out every tear and every ounce of frustration in a powerful prayer that resonates with women facing similar struggles today.

I've felt a fraction of what Hannah endured. After being diagnosed with fibroids and facing my own health challenges, there were days when my body felt like a battlefield. I'd look at other women who seemed to move effortlessly through life—conceiving children, glowing with health, or simply not carrying the same physical burdens—and I'd feel a pang of envy that I didn't want to admit was there. I've been provoked too, not always by rivals like Peninnah, but by whispers in my mind that said my body's struggles made me less worthy. But like Hannah, I learned to take that pain to God, to lay it bare in His presence, and to remember that my worth isn't tied to what my body can or cannot do.

The truth is that our bodies are incredible vessels, but they don't determine our worth. Modern culture places an enormous emphasis on physical capability—whether it's the ability to have children, meet beauty standards, or accomplish feats of strength. Women who don't fit neatly into these boxes are often made to feel less-than. But scripture tells us a different story. Hannah's inability to conceive didn't stop God from hearing her, loving her, or using her as part of His greater plan.

If you're struggling with infertility or other health challenges, know this: your spirit is strong, your heart is capable of love, and your life has a purpose beyond the limits of your body. Your worth isn't dictated by what society celebrates or what others deem valuable.

"WHEN POURING OUT YOUR HEART TO GOD, THE ONLY RULE IS NOT TO HOLD BACK!"

The Gem Being Dropped:

Your body doesn't define your worth. You are loved, cherished, and seen just as you are. God isn't looking at societal labels or limitations—He's looking straight into your heart. Hold onto that truth.

TIME TO DROP YOUR OWN GEMS:

♦ Hannah trusted God's timing even when her prayers felt unanswered. What are you currently waiting for in your life, and how can you find peace and purpose in the waiting season, even when it feels overwhelming?

♦ In what areas of your life are you expecting others, including your partner, to fill voids that only God can heal? How might embracing God's presence help you feel whole, even amid unmet desires?

♦ When was the last time you were truly vulnerable with God? What's holding you back from being fully transparent with Him, and how can you create a space for unfiltered honesty with God in your daily life?

♦ Are there areas where comparison with others has impacted your self-worth or joy? How can you redirect your focus to the unique journey God has for you?

- How have societal expectations or personal health challenges affected how you see your value? What affirmations or truths about your identity in Christ can you lean on to reclaim your worth?

- Hannah boldly vowed to dedicate her son to God. Have you ever made a vow or commitment to God in desperation? How might you return to those commitments, renewing them with intention now that time has passed?

- When Hannah finally received her blessing, she composed a song of praise. Reflect on a time when God answered a deep prayer of yours. How can you incorporate gratitude and praise into your life today, even if you still await certain blessings?

11

LESSONS FROM PENINNAH

Location: Peninnah lived in Ramah, in the hill country of Ephraim, alongside Elkanah and Hannah (1 Samuel 1:1-2).

RELATIONSHIP STATUS: POLYGAMOUS & PETTY

FAST FACTS:

- Peninnah's name means "pearl" or "coral." She is primarily known for her role in Hannah's story as her rival.
- Peninnah is remembered for taunting and provoking Hannah over her barrenness, creating tension within the family (1 Samuel 1:6-7).

LIFE EVENTS:

♦ Peninnah had children with Elkanah and often provoked Hannah due to her inability to conceive, leading to Hannah's deep distress (1 Samuel 1:6-7).

♦ Despite her provocations, Peninnah's presence in the story ultimately catalyzed Hannah's heartfelt prayer and Samuel's birth (1 Samuel 1:10-11).

THE WOMEN WHO CAN RELATE:

♦ Women in competitive relationships, especially within family dynamics, where jealousy and rivalry create emotional tension.

♦ Women who've felt overlooked or undervalued despite fulfilling traditional roles like motherhood or caregiving, leaving them with a sense of emptiness or lack.

♦ Women who struggle with insecurity and seek validation in relationships or through comparison with others.

♦ Women who've acted out of jealousy or pain and later regret the harm caused to their relationships, yearning for peace and healing.

♦ Women who've experienced conflict or bitterness rooted in favoritism, whether they were the favored one or the one left out.

♦ Women who've felt pressured to prove their worth or value in family or romantic relationships, often to their emotional detriment.

- Women who have used hurtful words or actions to mask their pain or insecurities, realizing the need for forgiveness and self-compassion.
- Women who've felt the strain of societal expectations, leading to unhealthy comparisons and rivalry with other women.
- Women who've realized the emotional toll of living in constant comparison and are now working toward finding joy and contentment in their unique journey.
- Women who've struggled with unmet emotional needs in relationships and are learning to address their pain while seeking personal growth and healing.

The Bible doesn't give us many details about Peninnah, but she is one of the two wives of Elkanah, a man from the tribe of Levi. The other wife is Hannah, who is famously barren. Peninnah, on the other hand, has children. This seemingly minor detail sets off a chain reaction of jealousy and pain in the narrative.

Peninnah is often cast as the story's villain, the stereotypical mean girl who delights in tormenting the less fortunate. However, a closer look at her character and the social context of her time reveals a more complex woman.

1

HURT PEOPLE HURT PEOPLE

"And her rival also provoked her severely, to make her miserable, because the Lord had closed her womb." (1 Samuel 1:6)

"Let all bitterness, wrath, anger, clamor, and evil speaking be put away from you, with all malice. And be kind to one another, tenderhearted, forgiving one another, even as God in Christ forgave you." (Ephesians 4:31-32)

I was the brunt of much bullying growing up. Children would tease me because I wore glasses and my teeth were crooked, which hadn't been corrected by braces. I even had girls glue my hair because they were jealous of my curl pattern. It wasn't fun at all. However, when I was older, I was able to confront some of my bullies. Through social media, we were able to connect, and I found the courage to ask them why they teased and bullied me as a child. Some deflected, but there's one woman who admitted she was having a hard time at home and in school and used bullying as a way to feel better about herself. She was hurting and thought hurting me would make her feel good. It didn't excuse the behavior, but it gave insight into why people use their words and actions to harm others intentionally.

Peninnah's taunting of Hannah is a prime example of this principle. Peninnah likely lived in a society that valued her primarily for her ability to bear children. This constant pressure to prove her worth could have bred insecurity and a need to feel superior. Hannah's barrenness may have allowed Peninnah to boost her ego. So, we find Peninnah bullying and inflicting pain on Hannah. It's a reminder that when women toss out ignorant, hurtful statements toward you, or when women write toxic, mean statements on social media, try not to take them personally. Many times, when people are hateful, it's because they're hurting themselves. It doesn't make it right, but it helps to remember not to make their bullying about you.

The Gem Being Dropped:

We've all been on the giving or receiving end of unkind words. When we are hurting, it's easy to lash out at others. But it's important to remember that true healing comes from addressing the root causes of our pain, not from inflicting pain on others.

"MANY TIMES, WHEN PEOPLE ARE HATEFUL, IT'S BECAUSE THEY'RE HURTING THEMSELVES."

2

FERTILITY DOESN'T DETERMINE YOUR WORTH

"But to Hannah he would give a double portion, for he loved Hannah, although the Lord had closed her womb." (1 Samuel 1:5)

A few years ago, we had an ant issue in our house, so we had to lay traps to catch them. Sure enough, they were lured to these traps, caught, and we eventually got rid of the persistent ants in our home. Believing our worth is tied to our productivity or accomplishments is a trap many fall into, especially if you are surrounded by an environment that praises your accomplishments more than who you are. In our achievement-focused society, it's easy to fall into the trap of believing that our value is connected to what we do. As Black women, we excel in many areas, but sometimes, society reduces our value to what we can achieve or produce.

Let's break free from that mindset. Peninnah reminds us that it's great to produce. It's a blessing to create, but it shouldn't be the bedrock and foundation from which we find our value and worth. As women of God, our worth is ultimately derived from God's love for us and simply existing. The Bible talks about our value coming from what God thinks of us more than from what we can do. No amount of productivity and accomplishments can make God love you any more than He already does. Paul told the Romans that "neither height nor depth nor anything else in all creation will be able to separate us from the love of God that is in Christ Jesus our Lord." (Romans 8:39). That includes your ability to produce and achieve great exploits. None of that will increase or decrease God's value in your life. Let's celebrate the many ways we excel and make a difference but never forget that our value is in who we are, not just what we do.

The Gem Being Dropped:

God created and loved you precisely as you are. Your worth is not dependent on your marital status, ability to have children, or career success.

"BELIEVING YOUR WORTH IS TIED TO WHAT YOU PRODUCE IS A TRAP DON'T FALL FOR IT."

3

HEAL, DON'T HARM

"Confess your trespasses to one another, and pray for one another, that you may be healed. The effective, fervent prayer of a righteous man avails much." (James 5:16)

Peninnah's actions in this story show us what happens when we choose not to allow God to heal our brokenness. She taunted Hannah from a place of hurt and jealousy. Just as an untreated wound can fester and cause pain to others, Peninnah's unresolved emotions led her to inflict pain on Hannah. Peninnah's inability to address her brokenness resulted in her lashing out. She did not allow God to heal her emotional wounds, which led to bitterness and cruelty. Just as an infected wound can spread, Peninnah's actions spread pain to Hannah, exacerbating her sorrow and longing. So, her story is a reminder to go through the healing process to stop bleeding on others with hurtful words and actions.

There's a Peninnah in us if we're unwilling to heal. We can end up hurting others or ourselves. Modern-day Penninah look like women who are mean girls, bullies, and bitter. They use their words to tear down instead of build up. They have come out of hurtful relationships with men and allowed those relationships to become the reason for being hateful to others and themselves. But just like physical wounds must heal, our hearts must heal so that we don't become a cesspool of hurt to others. It won't be easy. The first part of healing physical wounds is hemostasis. The blood vessels constrict to reduce bleeding, and platelets form a clot to seal the wound. That part can be painful. The initial pain can be intense and overwhelming. But you're allowed to permit yourself to begin the healing process just like the body immediately works to stop the bleeding, instead of allowing you to bleed over somebody else. Then, your wound experiences inflammation. White blood cells rush to the site to fight infection and remove debris. The area becomes red, swollen, and warm. The emotional "inflammation" will involve processing the pain and beginning to understand the depth of the hurt you've experienced. Again, this won't be an easy process. There will be discomfort and unease.

When our bodies experience this, there is redness and swelling. For you emotionally, there may be plenty of crying, anger, or even despair. But to heal completely, this part of the process must be endured to stop hurting others because of your pain. Then we have proliferation. Proliferation is the part of the process where new tissue and blood vessels form to replace what was damaged. The wound contracts as it heals. When you are healing emotionally, it will look like you are becoming a transformed person. You're slowly rebuilding yourself and becoming a new woman with a renewed sense of self and purpose.

You feel safe to shed the old you that was only trying to protect the wounded you. You find yourself slowly being able to replace the hurt with hope and the pain with praise. This takes time, but you will get there. The final phase of healing is the maturation phase. This is my favorite part. The wound continues to strengthen, and scar tissue forms. The area regains some normal function, though it may look different than before. When we heal emotionally, we are never the same, but we have emotional scars to remind us of our journey. The wounds never go away, but the healing remains. The scars keep us from hurting others because we remember what it was like to be hurt by someone else. So, I believe Peninnah's story reminds us of the importance of healing so that our pain isn't weaponized against others.

The Gem Being Dropped:

You deserve the healing process; you owe it to yourself and others to heal from who and what hurt you.

"THERE'S A PENINNAH IN ALL OF US IF WE REFUSE TO HEAL!"

POLYGAMOUS RELATIONSHIPS DON'T WORK WHEN JEALOUSY IS INVOLVED.

"For where envy and self-seeking exist, confusion and every evil thing are there." (James 3:16)

This section is not for or against polygamy. As a sex educator, I've been trained and exposed to an assortment of relationships and understand why people opt for these relationships, either for cultural, religious, or societal reasons. God has an ideal, yes, and I'm also aware that many women of faith love God deeply and are in relationships that could be classified as polygamous. Elkanah's relationship with his two wives is a cautionary tale about the dark side of any relationship that doesn't have security and love as a strong foundation.

The competition between Hannah and Peninnah created a toxic environment for everyone involved. Peninnah constantly taunted Hannah, and even though Elkanah professed his love for Hannah, the imbalance in affection and the lack of resolution between the two women only made matters worse. This kind of environment doesn't just harm the individuals directly involved; it affects the entire household. Jealousy and envy fester in silence but erupt in ways that can fracture trust, respect, and intimacy.

Polygamy isn't demonized or vilified in this text, but jealousy and envy are. And if jealousy and envy happen in monogamous relationships, imagine how much more complex they can become in polygamous ones. One of my clients shared her story about being in a polyamorous relationship where jealousy wasn't discussed beforehand. She thought she was okay with sharing her partner's attention, but as time passed, she found herself feeling left out during significant moments, like holidays and anniversaries. Instead of addressing her feelings, she internalized them, which eventually led to resentment and the eventual breakdown of the relationship. Her story is a reminder that even unconventional relationships require honesty, communication, and boundaries to succeed.

It doesn't mean that polygamy must be explored or endorsed. Still, I think this story does provide caution about entering into any relationship with emotional and spiritual maturity to manage negative emotions that come to the surface. You can't be a jealous person and be in a relationship with someone. There has to be a healthy security to trust who you are with. And if a jealous emotion emerges, you must have the courage to address it. Speak openly with your partner to establish clarity, reassurance, and perhaps even a course correction if necessary.

The Gem Being Dropped

God's design for marriage is a monogamous relationship between one man and one woman. If you're considering entering into a polygamous relationship, it's important to weigh the risks carefully, just like you would in a monogamous relationship. If you know you get jealous quickly, relationships might not be right for you until you've done the work—perhaps through therapy or intentional self-reflection—to address those feelings.

5

FORGIVE YOURSELF FOR WHAT YOU DID TO EARN LOVE.

> *"As far as the east is from the west, so far has He removed our transgressions from us." Psalm 103:12*
>
> *(NKJV)*

We all have our stories. Whether cutting our hair, dying our hair, listening to music we hated, moving to a new city, cooking for them, laughing at jokes we didn't find funny, ignoring red flags, changing our wardrobe, or changing ourselves. We all have stories of what we have done to earn a man's love, attention, and adoration. I remember watching the Elvis movie that portrayed all his wife Priscilla did to appease Elvis. She changed her hair color, wore blue dresses just for him, and wore dress styles that he liked while ignoring or minimizing what she wanted.

Likewise, Peninnah's actions may have been fueled by a deep-seated insecurity about her worth. She may have believed that having children was the only way to secure her husband's love. This is a common insecurity that many women face, even today. We have women who are insecure about who they are, so they try to earn the love and attention of a man.

There's no judgment here, though. I want us to forgive ourselves for the lengths that we went to be loved. It doesn't mean you're weak. It doesn't mean you're a problem. It doesn't mean you're a terrible person. It means that deep down, you know you deserve to be loved deeply and cared for, and you were trying to convince a man of that truth. That's all you are guilty of - trying to convince someone of what you already know to be true - that you're terrific, deserving, and worthy of love. Forgive yourself for trying to make others see your worth. Forgive yourself for trying to make others see your beauty and value. Forgive yourself for all the times you tried to make someone love you. Turn that energy towards yourself now and go forward. The right man will come along, and you won't have to prove anything to them.

The Gem Being Dropped:

You are worthy of love, just as you are. Don't give your power away to anyone by trying to earn their love.

TIME TO DROP YOUR OWN GEMS:

- Have you ever felt pressure to conform to societal expectations about what makes a woman worthy? How can you challenge those expectations and embrace your worth in God's eyes?

- Do you ever find yourself comparing yourself to other women? How can you cultivate a spirit of love and support for other women rather than competition?

- How does your faith inform your view of relationships? What are your boundaries in a relationship, and how can you communicate them effectively?

- Think about a time when you responded to pain by hurting someone else. How can you learn from that experience and choose forgiveness and healing instead?

- What does true love look like to you? How can you cultivate healthy, fulfilling relationships based on love, respect, and open communication?

_____

_____

_____

_____

_____

_____

_____

_____

_____

_____

_____

_____

12

LESSONS FROM BATHSHEBA

Location: Bathsheba lived in Jerusalem, the capital of Israel, during King David's reign. (2 Samuel 11:2-4, 2 Samuel 12:24).

RELATIONSHIP STATUS: TAKEN

FAST FACTS:

◆ Bathsheba was bathing on a rooftop when King David saw her and lusted after her (2 Samuel 11:2).

◆ Solomon, her son with David, became one of the most fabulous kings in Israel's history and was part of the genealogical line leading to Jesus (Matthew 1:6).

◆ Bathsheba later played a crucial role in securing the throne for her son Solomon (1 Kings 1:11-31).

LIFE EVENTS:

- Bathsheba was summoned by King David, who committed adultery with her while her husband Uriah was at war (2 Samuel 11:4).
- After becoming pregnant, David arranged for Uriah's death in battle to cover up the affair (2 Samuel 11:14-17).
- Nathan, the prophet, confronted David, leading to David's repentance, but their first child together died as a consequence of David's sin (2 Samuel 12:1-19).
- Bathsheba later became the mother of Solomon, and her wisdom and influence are seen in the later stages of David's reign (1 Kings 1:11-31).

THE WOMEN WHO CAN RELATE:

- Women who have been caught in the crossfire of powerful men's decisions, especially when they had little agency.
- Women who have experienced loss after being involved in complicated relationships.
- Women who have experienced the loss of loved ones due to murder.
- Women who have experienced the loss of a baby.
- Women who've been able to use their position to advocate for their children or ensure a secure future for them.

Bathsheba's story in the Bible is one of the most captivating and complex. She's often reduced to a footnote in David's narrative—a beautiful woman who sparked a king's dark desires. Many of us have heard Bathsheba's story whispered in hushed tones, maybe even internalized some judgment. Was she a temptress who lured David astray? Was she a passive pawn in a powerful man's game? We must continue to say her name beyond being a problem for David. In this chapter, let's reclaim her narrative and see the gems waiting to be unearthed for our lives, love, and relationships. We'll see that Bathsheba wasn't responsible for David's choices, and her story offers powerful lessons about healing from the fallout of the mistakes of another.

The Bible describes Bathsheba as beautiful, a word that likely meant more than just physical appearance back then. It could signify her virtue, fertility, or social standing. Regardless, her beauty caught the eye of a powerful king, and that's where things got messy.

YOU CANNOT CONTROL THE LUST ISSUES OF MEN

> *"Then it happened one evening that David arose from his bed and walked on the roof of the king's house. And from the roof he saw a woman bathing, and the woman was very beautiful to behold." 2 Samuel 11:2*

> *"Then David sent messengers, and took her; and she came to him, and he lay with her, for she was cleansed from her impurity; and she returned to her house." (2 Samuel 11:4)*

> *"But each one is tempted when he is drawn away by his own desires and enticed. Then, when desire has conceived, it gives birth to sin; and sin, when it is full-grown, brings forth death." (James 1:14-15)*

Bathsheba doesn't say much, but her body speaks for itself. She was a beautiful woman. However, her body language did not request or suggest that it be used or taken without her consent. When King

David saw her, she was enjoying some innocent "me time" on the rooftop. She wasn't out there with a flashing neon sign saying, "Come hither, Your Majesty!" David, a man with plenty of power and a not-so-great track record when it comes to women, is the one who makes the sinful choice. Bathsheba had no control over his wandering eye or his abuse of power. Her beauty was not an invitation or excuse for David's objectification and forced sexual interaction.

I think of remote-controlled cars and how they need a remote to control their every move. The car goes where it's told. This is how David treated Bathsheba. Like a toy car he could control. The Hebrew language suggests that she had no choice when the messengers came and took her to David. She didn't have a choice once she got to the king's chamber because he was powerful. Be clear: just because she went to his palace doesn't mean she consented to an encounter in the palace with him.

Can you think of places or situations you ended up in that you didn't want to experience? Then you're in the same company as Bathsheba. She ended up in this predicament mainly because David had issues. Serious issues. He was a man who lacked control and discipline when it came to women. David is the one who collected women as if they were baseball cards and discarded them because of his lust issues. Bathsheba reminds us that we do not have the capacity or power, nor should we have the desire, to control the urges and desires of men. Bathsheba could've taken a shower in a waterproof dress, and he still would've scooped her up without her permission because of the issues within his soul. The onus will forever be on David and his control issues. Lust is not about attraction. It's about envy, jealousy, and control.

The Gem Being Dropped:

We have to internalize this. Men are responsible for their own actions and desires. We can't contort ourselves into pretzels trying to avoid tempting a man who can't control himself. Our worth is not defined by whether or not we accidentally spark a man's lust. We are worthy, desirable, and deserving of respect, regardless of what someone else might project onto us.

2

DON'T TAKE ON SEXUAL GUILT THAT DOESN'T BELONG TO YOU

"So David said to Nathan, 'I have sinned against the Lord.' And Nathan said to David, 'The Lord also has put away your sin; you shall not die." (2 Samuel 12:13)

"Have mercy upon me, O God, according to Your lovingkindness; according to the multitude of Your tender mercies, blot out my transgressions. Wash me thoroughly from my iniquity, and cleanse me from my sin. For I acknowledge my transgressions, and my sin is always before me. Against You, You only, have I sinned, and done this evil in Your sight." (Psalm 51:1-4)

Bathsheba sleeping with David does not at all prove agreement or desire for David. There was no reason for her to feel guilty. There was an immense power imbalance here. Similar to a seesaw or teeter-totter where children balance on either side, there was an imbalance with David being up top and Bathsheba being at a considerable loss.

David is the King. Bathsehba's a subject. The story doesn't suggest she had any real say in the matter. She was most likely pressured, coerced, or even afraid to refuse the king's advances. Yet, sometimes, the narrative gets twisted, and Bathsheba carries the burden of guilt. Bathsheba shows us that It wasn't her fault, and it wasn't your fault, either. Nathan went to King David, not her, and said YOU are the man.

David was a man who represented power, religious authority, institutional control, and political dominion. And he was the one guilty. She was innocent in all of this. Even when the baby was created and lost, Bathsheba was not responsible. It wasn't her fault that this whole situation happened in the first place.

Many women carry sexual shame over abusive situations they didn't ask for. The guilt is also amplified when the abuser is a person of power and prestige. Because now they feel like they've ruined their abusers' lives for coming forward or getting pregnant. But again, the emphasis must always be placed on the man who decided to send his messengers to go for you. It wasn't your fault. Some women feel guilty because they were aroused and seemingly enjoyed the encounter. Understand that our bodies have biological, natural responses to stimuli, even in unwanted situations. And our bodies will also protect us by becoming aroused so it doesn't feel as painful. So again, it's not on you to feel guilty about a forced sexual encounter even if you got wet and "turned on."

Even in my own life, I had to release the guilt and shame I felt from being exploited and abused because I was accused of being fast and loose. The perception of women being responsible for their sexual trauma is an old trick of the enemy. Please don't fall for it. It wasn't your fault.

"NATHAN WENT TO KING DAVID, NOT HER, AND SAID YOU ARE THE MAN."

The Gem Being Dropped:

If you've ever been in a situation where you were pressured into something sexual, you don't own that guilt. It belongs to the person who violated your boundaries. This might be tough to unpack, but trust me, you are worthy of healthy, consensual relationships. Don't let someone else's shame steal your joy.

3

YOU WILL RECOVER FROM SEXUAL ABUSE

"Bathsheba therefore went to King Solomon, to speak to him for Adonijah. And the king rose up to meet her and bowed down to her, and sat down on his throne and had a throne set for the king's mother; so she sat at his right hand." (1 Kings 2:19)

"Instead of your shame you shall have double honor, and instead of confusion they shall rejoice in their portion. Therefore in their land they shall possess double; everlasting joy shall be theirs." (Isaiah 61:7)

When I was young, I had this little collection of erasers—not the boring brown ones but the kind that looked like strawberries, cherries, or those bright white erasers that could erase mistakes completely. I was, you could say, an eraser connoisseur. I loved the idea that a mistake, a wrong word, or a crooked sentence could disappear. I know we can't erase our past. But just like we rewrote sentences with those erasers, we can rewrite the narratives of our lives.

Bathsheba shows us that it's possible to rise as a thriving survivor instead of being forever defined by victimhood.

When we get to 1 Kings 2:19, Bathsheba steps into her role as the queen mother, no longer merely a victim of David's abuse. I can imagine her journey was anything but easy. Perhaps there were days she wished she had perished with Uriah. Yet, Bathsheba not only survived—she thrived. The scripture tells us Solomon's throne was firmly established, and right beside him sat his mother, Bathsheba. This is the woman who had been taken, violated, and silenced. The woman who had no say in her imbalanced relationship with David. Yet she survived, endured, and rose to a place of dignity and respect, seated as a queen.

I know there are thrones you will sit upon—thrones of confidence, joy, and authority— as a radiant queen despite the pain or trauma that might sit in your past. There is no abuse, no violation, no exploitation that defines you or can strip you of your worth. You are worthy of rewriting your story, reclaiming your power, and sitting where you are meant to rule. Your agency and autonomy can be restored through your strength and the support of those around you who hand you an eraser and a pen. Bathsheba had Solomon and Nathan, pivotal men who helped her reclaim her place.

Bathsheba's story shows us that healing from sexual abuse is possible and, even more, that it is your right. There is a throne of dignity, purpose, and power for you to sit on, far from the shame or confusion that trauma might have left behind. And though healing may not be easy, you are strong, worthy, and deserving of a bright future. No one is defined by what happened to them. Like Bathsheba, you are a survivor—and a queen whose story is still unfolding.

The Gem Being Dropped:

This is a reminder that healing from sexual abuse is possible. It won't be easy, but you are strong, worthy, and capable of overcoming this pain. There is no shame in seeking help and support. You are not defined by what happened to you. You are a survivor, and your future is bright.

4

GOD DID NOT NEED TO HAVE YOU ABUSED FOR YOU TO BE ANOINTED.

"Then David comforted Bathsheba his wife, and went in to her and lay with her. So she bore a son, and he called his name Solomon. Now the Lord loved him." (2 Samuel 12:24)

"And we know that all things work together for good to those who love God, to those who are the called according to His purpose." (Romans 8:28)

This is a crucial point to remember in Bathsheba's story. I've heard preachers say that Solomon wouldn't have been born and the lineage of Jesus wouldn't have happened the way it did had Bathsheba not been with David. It's been said that everything works together for the good of those who love God. Everything happens for a reason, and God can take ugly things and make them beautiful in his time. This is an infuriating, irresponsible perspective of the story. Yes, God can take the most heinous, most disgusting, most broken parts of our story and make something beautiful that brings God glory and honor despite what's happened to us. But God does not NEED those horrible things to have happened to us for us to be elevated, promoted, or go to another level in God. There's this pervasive idea in Christianity that God needed you to go through bad things to make you more anointed and powerful. You had to go through the fire to come out as pure gold, and you needed to suffer to come out stronger and better. Sis. No. I want us to be free from that.

You did not NEED to be abused. You did not NEED to be raped. You did not NEED to be exploited. You did not NEED to be assaulted. You did not NEED David to come and ruin your life so that God could get the glory. God could get the glory out of your life minus the drama, trauma, abuse, and pain. Indeed, Bathsheba would not have had Solomon if David had not taken her from Uriah. Indeed, she would not have had this life. But we will never know what kind of life she and Uriah would have had. We will never know what her children with Uriah would've looked like. We will never know what kind of wife she could've been to Uriah in their older years. We will never know what kind of life they could've had after he returned from war. We will never know. That's something to mourn and grieve deeply. That's not something to brush to the side and say, "Oh, it simply wasn't God's will. Living in a sinful world doesn't remove the pain, heartache, and brokenness of living in a sinful world. So yes, God can use bad things for our good, but I promise it didn't have to happen that way. Sin happened that way, not God.

"YOU DID NOT NEED TO BE ABUSED. YOU DID NOT NEED TO BE RAPED. YOU DID NOT NEED TO BE EXPLOITED."

The Gem Being Dropped:

God doesn't need you to go through a mess to be pretty and powerful. While God can take messy circumstances and create something beautiful, such events aren't always necessary for God's purpose in our lives.

5

HONOR YOUR LOVE, RELEASE THE SHAME

"David therefore pleaded with God for the child, and David fasted and went in and lay all night on the ground. So the elders of his house arose and went to him, to raise him from the ground; but he would not, nor did he eat food with them." (2 Samuel 12:16-17)

"And God will wipe away every tear from their eyes; there shall be no more death, nor sorrow, nor crying. There shall be no more pain, for the former things have passed away." (Revelation 21:4)

Bathsheba's story speaks to a resilience many women carry in silence. She lived through the complexity of loss, betrayal, and powerlessness yet emerged with quiet strength. Her story is one of survival, honor, and deep inner courage. Bathsheba knows the weight of grief, especially when that grief is tangled with violation and heartache. She knows the challenge of grieving a child born of sorrow. For mothers who bear this burden, Bathsheba's words extend as a compassionate hand, a reminder that grief shared can help with grief being softened.

This imagined letter is Bathsheba's offering to those who've lost a child conceived in pain yet cherished with love. It's an invitation to feel, grieve, and hope again. Through Bathsheba's letter, let her strength guide you; her words remind you that you're not alone, and her story encourages you on your lifelong journey of healing.

Dearest Sister,

My heart feels the weight you're carrying—deeper than words could ever express. Losing a child is a pain that changes everything. And to have that loss tangled with violation, with injustice—it's more than anyone should ever have to bear. I know a taste of that darkness, the kind that feels like it's trying to pull you under and suffocate you.

When David stole from me what should have been a moment of pure joy, it left me with wounds that ran deep. The shame, the guilt—they clung to me, almost as if it was my fault. But sister, you carry an even heavier weight. This beautiful and innocent child wasn't a symbol of love but a reminder of something so deeply wrong. And yet, the love you poured out? That was real. That love grew in you, pure and strong, even when it felt impossible.

So, let the tears fall. Don't hold back your grief; don't silence your heartbreak. Mourn what was stolen, grieve the dreams that shattered. But as you do, don't lose sight of the love. Remember the little kicks, the whispers in the quiet moments. That love you felt for your child? It was real and still burns, and it's a light that'll carry you through this valley.

Yes, weeping may last through this long night, but joy will come again in the morning. This pain won't vanish instantly, but it will soften. Let your memories be a comfort, not a torment. Hold on to the love for your child—not the pain of how they came to be.

And know this: you are a warrior. You've walked through a nightmare, and yet here you are. You're still standing, fierce and unbreakable. Lean on those who love you and who see your strength beyond the pain. And if your faith brings comfort, let it hold you. Know that this child, though not in your arms, is sleeping peacefully until Jesus returns.

This journey will be long, and healing won't come overnight. But sister, you are not alone. I am walking beside you as someone who's been through the depths and come back with scars—but still whole. You are a mother and that fierce love you have? Let it be your anchor, your light guiding you through.

With all the love in my heart,
Bathsheba

TIME TO DROP YOUR OWN GEMS:

- Have you ever felt judged or blamed for a man's inappropriate behavior? How can you challenge those feelings and reclaim your sense of worth?

- Think about healthy boundaries in relationships. What are some ways you can communicate your needs and desires clearly?

- Have you ever experienced a situation where you felt pressured into something sexual? How did it make you feel? What resources are available to help you heal?

- Think about a time you've experienced loss. How did you find strength and hope to move forward?

- Reflect on the concept of forgiveness. Is it something you need to extend to yourself or someone else? How can you find peace and healing through forgiveness?

_____

_____

_____

_____

_____

_____

_____

_____

_____

_____

_____

_____

_____

13

LESSONS FROM TAMAR (DAVID'S DAUGHTER)

Location: Tamar lived in Jerusalem, in the royal household of King David, during his reign over Israel. (2 Samuel 13:20)

RELATIONSHIP STATUS: SINGLE BY FORCE

FAST FACTS:

- Tamar was known for her beauty and was described as wearing a richly ornamented robe, the attire of a king's virgin daughter (2 Samuel 13:18).
- Tamar's name means "palm tree," a symbol of beauty and grace in ancient Hebrew culture.
- Her tragic story of assault was one of the catalysts for her brother Absalom's rebellion against their father, King David (2 Samuel 13:28-29).

LIFE EVENTS:

- Tamar was deceived and assaulted by her half-brother Amnon, who pretended to be ill to lure her into his room (2 Samuel 13:6-14).

- After the assault, Amnon rejected her, causing further emotional devastation.

- In her grief, she tore her robe and put ashes on her head (2 Samuel 13:15-19).

- Tamar's brother Absalom took her into his house, but her life after the incident remained one of isolation and grief (2 Samuel 13:20).

- Absalom later killed Amnon as revenge for what he did to Tamar, sparking family turmoil (2 Samuel 13:28-29).

THE WOMEN WHO CAN RELATE:

- Women who have experienced sexual assault or trauma, and the emotional devastation that follows.

- Women who have experienced sexual assault or trauma and are working to reclaim their self-worth and identity beyond what was taken from them.

♦ Women who've felt betrayed by family or trusted individuals and left to navigate the aftermath of shame, isolation, and grief alone.

♦ Women who've been pressured to stay silent about their pain to protect family or societal image, yet yearn to speak their truth.

♦ Women who've struggled to find justice, feeling abandoned or invalidated by systems or individuals meant to protect them.

♦ Women who carry the weight of generational trauma and are determined to heal so the cycle ends with them.

♦ Women who've been labeled "troublesome" or "dramatic" for standing up for their boundaries or speaking out about their abuse.

♦ Women who understand the value of sisterhood and support, finding strength in safe spaces where their truth is honored without judgment.

Open your Bible to 2 Samuel 13, and you'll meet Tamar, daughter of King David—a woman whose story is often whispered about but deserves to be shouted from the rooftops. Tamar's story isn't just a tragic account; it's a testament to resilience, sisterhood, and hope for every woman who's ever been violated.

Let's be honest—her story is heavy. It's about betrayal and unspeakable harm by someone she should've been able to trust. But, Tamar's story isn't just about shame. It's about rediscovering your power when the world tries to dim your light.

In Tamar's time, women were property, valued for bearing children and securing alliances. Speaking out against a powerful man risked everything. Yet Tamar's story whispers of strength that defies the odds.

RAPE STEALS YOUR IDENTITY, BUT YOU GET TO TAKE IT BACK

> *"Now she had on a robe of many colors, for the king's virgin daughters wore such apparel... Tamar put ashes on her head and tore her robe of many colors... and went away crying bitterly." (2 Samuel 13:18-19)*

> *"To console those who mourn in Zion, to give them beauty for ashes, the oil of joy for mourning, the garment of praise for the spirit of heaviness..." (Isaiah 61:3)*

Tamar's story begins with a brutal truth – her half-brother, Amnon, rapes her. In that horrific act, Amnon attempts to steal not just her physical body but her sense of self. Her identity switched from being celebrated for her beauty to being violated for her beauty. Her own brother didn't see her as a woman to be cherished but as a receptacle to be used. She ripped the dress that she wore because her dress symbolized her identity as a virgin, and she knew she couldn't bring herself to wear it anymore because her identity was taken.

This, my sisters, is a reality that far too many women know. The violation of rape shatters your world, leaving you feeling broken and questioning your worth. But here's the powerful takeaway: Rape does not have to define you.

You can reteach your mind to love yourself again. You can reteach your mind to see yourself as valuable and worthy of love even though someone tried to rob it from you. Some may not know this, but I'm a classically trained pianist, though I don't practice like I used to. So when I went home, I said, "Let me dust off some of this Beethoven and Chopin." But I had to reteach the arpeggios and scales to my fingers because it had been a while. And for some of us, when we find ourselves on the other side of being used, stepped on, abused, or violated, we have to reteach ourselves who we are by speaking the Word of God over our lives. After experiencing sexual assault, here are some scriptures you can speak over yourself:

"HER IDENTITY SWITCHED FROM BEING CELEBRATED FOR HER BEAUTY TO BEING VIOLATED FOR HER BEAUTY."

Speak These Truths Over Yourself

- John 15:16 – You are chosen
- Galatians 4:7 – You are free
- 1 John 1:9 – You are forgiven
- 2 Corinthians 5:17 – You are a new person
- John 1:12 – You are a child of God
- Genesis 1:27 – You are made in God's image
- 1 Corinthians 3:23 – You belong to Jesus
- Romans 6:4 – Jesus offers you a new life
- Philippians 3:20 – You are a citizen of Heaven
- 1 Peter 1:5 – You are protected by God
- 1 Corinthians 12:27 – You are part of something important
- Romans 8:38-39 – God loves you no matter what
- Zephaniah 3:17 – God is with you
- Psalm 139:13-16 – You are God's special creation
- Isaiah 43:4 – You are precious to God
- Galatians 3:13 – You are rescued
- Jeremiah 29:11 – God has a plan for your life
- 1 John 5:14-15 – God listens to you
- Philippians 4:13 – God gives you strength
- Romans 8:17 – You are an heir of God
- Ephesians 2:19 – You are part of God's family
- Romans 10:13 – You are saved
- 1 Corinthians 6:19 – The Holy Spirit lives in you
- Psalm 23:1-3 – God is taking care of you

- John 15:11 – Jesus gives you true joy
- Ephesians 1:3 – You are blessed
- Galatians 2:20 – Jesus gave himself for you
- Psalm 139:1 – God understands you
- Exodus 19:5 – You are treasured by God
- Colossians 2:10 – You are complete in Christ

You are not your trauma. You are a woman of strength, resilience, and survivor.

The Gem Being Dropped:

What happened to you doesn't have to claim who you are entirely. It happened and you can arise from it. You are worthy of love, respect, and wholeness. No matter what you've been through, your capacity to love and be loved remains.

2

DO NOT BE SILENCED BY SHAME. SPEAK YOUR TRUTH

> *"And Absalom her brother said to her, 'Has Amnon your brother been with you? But now hold your peace, my sister. He is your brother; do not take this thing to heart.' So Tamar remained desolate in her brother Absalom's house." (2 Samuel 13:20)*

> *"Open your mouth, judge righteously, And plead the cause of the poor and needy." (Proverbs 31:9)*

Absalom abused his relationship with Tamar by silencing her truth. In doing so, he not only denied her the opportunity to express her pain but compounded her suffering. His words, "Hold your peace," were not meant to comfort Tamar but to protect their family's reputation. This betrayal of trust is painfully familiar to many women who have been silenced by societal, cultural, or familial pressures, particularly within faith communities.

Part of the reason I was diagnosed with heart failure was because

I was struggling to breathe. And one thing is for sure: it's hard to pretend you're not struggling to breathe when you actually are. This is what happened to Tamar. She wasn't given space to exhale the weight of her trauma. Absalom essentially told her, "Keep quiet. We're the royal family. Don't let this become a scandal." But it's impossible to heal from pain when you're suffocating under the pressure of silence.

In many Christian circles, when it comes to our abuse, we're taught to ignore it. To spiritualize it. To drown it. To placate it. To pacify it. To hold it together. I remember sitting in a church meeting years ago, listening to a young woman share her testimony of surviving an abusive relationship. Instead of receiving encouragement, she was met with questions about how she might have contributed to the situation. It was devastating to watch her retreat into herself, the shame written across her face. That moment made it clear to me how much work we have to do in creating spaces where women feel safe to speak their truth.

To someone dealing with deep-rooted pain or trauma, Tamar's story is a reminder that even when she didn't have the agency or strength to speak up, we do today. Her pain calls out to us, urging us to break the silence. Speak up through journaling; pour your emotions onto the page where no one can judge. Speak up by talking to a counselor who is trained to hold space for your healing. Speak up through trusted friendships, finding people who will listen without shame or judgment. Express yourself through the arts—paint, write poetry, or dance to reclaim what was taken from you. Or share with a trusted pastor who can guide you with compassion and care.

Silence is not your destiny. Shame thrives in the dark, but healing begins when we bring our pain into the light.

The Gem Being Dropped:

Don't let shame silence you. Your voice matters. Find a safe space, a sisterhood, a therapist—whoever you need—and speak your truth. Sharing your story can be incredibly liberating. You are not alone. There are people who believe in you and want to support you.

3

FIND PEOPLE WHO BELIEVE YOU AND BUILD YOUR SUPPORT SYSTEM

"And Absalom her brother said to her, 'Has Amnon your brother been with you? But now hold your peace, my sister. He is your brother; do not take this thing to heart.' So Tamar remained desolate in her brother Absalom's house." (2 Samuel 13:20)

"Bear one another's burdens, and so fulfill the law of Christ." (Galatians 6:2)

In the aftermath of her assault, Tamar finds herself isolated. David, her father, fails to deliver justice, leaving her feeling unheard and alone. She has daddy issues because King David chose not to speak up for her when she was abused. David was present but his silence made him absent and made her feel abandoned. King David is powerful to defend this city but not powerful enough to protect me? David is quick to run to Amnon's bedside when he's sick but not do anything for me when I'm sick with sorrow and grief?

Perhaps King Daddy David to Tamar felt like his indiscretions with Bathsheba bridled his tongue from calling out Amnon on his bad decisions. We can't say for sure. But it's likely that Tamar felt like saying, "When I needed my daddy, he wasn't there!" The way David was acting, David might as well have been in the room restraining her when the incident happened because his anger didn't propel him to action. Tamar's story resonates with so many of us because we were let down by people who were a LOUD spiritual authority but were silent on our issues and pain.

You had people who didn't show up for you the way you needed when you were going through it. There wasn't a strong support system. They were accusatory, cautious, slow to believe you, and quick to defend your abuser. Tamar sees you, woman of God. She sees how painful it is to look to family and friends that you thought would be there, but fall short. As you seek to pick up the pieces of your life after you have experienced harm, feel empowered to build or rebuild your support system.

Surround yourself with people who will believe you, advocate for you and celebrate your journey to healing. You don't have to walk this path alone.

The Gem Being Dropped:

Build a support system of people who believe in you and will advocate for you. This could be a trusted friend, therapist, support group, or even a hotline. Feel free to reach out for help. Having a solid support system provides a safe space to process your experiences, rebuild your confidence, and find strength.

Remember, sisterhood is powerful. Lean on the women who uplift and empower you.

4

NO STILL MEANS NO: THE POWER OF CONSENT

"Now when she had brought them to him to eat, he took hold of her and said to her, 'Come, lie with me, my sister.' But she answered him, 'No, my brother, do not force me, for no such thing should be done in Israel!'" (2 Samuel 13:11-12)

"Whoever has no rule over his own spirit is like a city broken down, without walls." (Proverbs 25:28)

The core of Tamar's story revolves around the violation of consent. Amnon ignores her pleas, her tears, her clear and present "no." Tamar's voice rings loud and clear as she pleads with Amnon, her brother, to honor her dignity and her autonomy. She says no again—clearly, firmly, and repeatedly—but her words fall on deaf ears. Her "no" is not just ignored; it is trampled underfoot by a culture of entitlement and power. But Tamar reminds us that even if you're completely naked, in a man's bed and decide to change your mind about a sexual encounter - no still means no. If you were intoxicated wearing a plunging neckline and a short skirt, your no still means no. If you were wearing leggings and a crop top while taking a run in your neighborhood - your no still means no. If you're married and don't feel like having sex with your spouse - your no matters and your no still means no!

The pervasive mindset that allows excuses for violating consent—based on what someone was wearing, doing, or where they were—is one of the cornerstones of rape culture. By perpetuating these toxic ideas, we create a world where boundaries are blurred and accountability is erased. Tamar's story shows us the stark reality of what happens when consent is disregarded, and it challenges us to confront the systems and mindsets that enable such violations to continue.

It's also crucial to note the connection between consent and self-control. Proverbs 25:28 paints a vivid picture: "Whoever has no rule over his own spirit is like a city broken down, without walls." This verse reminds us that the responsibility to respect boundaries is not on the person setting them but on the person receiving them. Amnon's lack of self-control led to the devastation of Tamar's life and, ultimately, his own downfall. The inability to respect a "no" reflects a lack of discipline, integrity, and respect for God's design for human relationships.

The Gem Being Dropped:

Consent is still beautiful, sacred and yes, even sexy. It's the foundation for healthy, respectful relationships. Learn to communicate your boundaries clearly and unapologetically. A true partner will respect your "no" every single time. Remember, your body is your temple. You have the right to say no to anything that doesn't feel good, no matter the circumstances. Don't be afraid to assert yourself.

TIME TO DROP YOUR OWN GEMS:

- Have you ever felt that a painful experience redefined you in ways you didn't choose? What would reclaiming your identity look like in this season of your life?

- Have there been times when shame or fear stopped you from speaking your truth? What steps could you take to create a safe space where you can express yourself openly?

- Who has been present for you during your most challenging times, and where have you felt let down? How can you intentionally build or strengthen a circle of support that respects and believes in you?

- Tamar's story emphasizes the importance of consent and the right to say "no." Reflect on a time when your boundaries were ignored. How can you start honoring your own boundaries today, and what would that look like in both new and existing relationships?

◆ If you've ever felt pressured to stay silent about your pain, how might you begin sharing your story—whether through journaling, art, or a trusted conversation? What do you need to feel safe and empowered as you start to open up?

◆ Tamar's story reminds us that we are not our trauma. In what ways have you been holding onto past pain that no longer serves you? What affirmations or reminders could help you reconnect with the truth of who you are beyond those painful moments?

◆ Think about the women in your life who may also be carrying pain. How can you support them, offering the kind of compassionate listening and advocacy that Tamar needed? What would it look like to create a sisterhood rooted in love, understanding, and empowerment?

14

LESSONS
FROM
DELILAH

Location: Delilah lived in the Valley of Sorek, an area near the border of Israelite and Philistine territory (Judges 16:4).

RELATIONSHIP STATUS: SINGLE

FAST FACTS:

- Delilah is not described as Samson's wife, but rather as a woman he loved.
- She is infamous for being the woman who betrayed Samson, leading to his capture by the Philistines (Judges 16:18-21).
- Delilah's name has become synonymous with betrayal and deceit in popular culture.

LIFE EVENTS:

- The Philistine rulers bribed Delilah to discover the secret of Samson's strength in exchange for a large sum of money (Judges 16:5).
- After several failed attempts, Delilah finally got Samson to reveal that his strength lay in his uncut hair, symbolizing his Nazirite vow (Judges 16:15-17).
- Delilah cut Samson's hair while he slept, rendering him powerless, and handed him over to the Philistines, who captured and blinded him (Judges 16:18-21).

WOMEN WHO CAN RELATE

- Women who've navigated relationships with complex power dynamics, especially where betrayal or manipulation played a role.
- Women who've made decisions out of necessity, only to face judgment or condemnation for doing what they thought was best.
- Women who've been misunderstood, labeled negatively, or villainized for their strength, independence, or self-sufficiency.

- ◆ Women who've leveraged their influence in relationships, sometimes for personal gain, and now grapple with the consequences.

- ◆ Women who recognize the damage caused by unhealthy alliances and are ready to break free from choices that no longer serve them.

- ◆ Women who are tired of love games and crave connections built on honesty, peace, and mutual respect.

- ◆ Women who are reclaiming their narrative, breaking stereotypes, and redefining their identity unapologetically.

Have you ever winced at the name Delilah? She's often painted as a conniving temptress who betrayed Samson, but what if there's more to her story?

Delilah, introduced in Judges 16, wasn't just Samson's lover—she was a Philistine woman living in a land hostile to Israel. Her identity wasn't tied to a man but to survival in a violent, patriarchal society. In her world, women were often seen as property, their value tied to their ability to bear children and manage households.

The Philistines offered Delilah a hefty sum to uncover Samson's secret. Was it manipulation? Maybe. But in a world offering her so few options, can we blame her for using the tools she had?

Delilah's story isn't black and white. It's a tale of survival that reveals women's vulnerabilities in systems of power and the complexities of love, loyalty, and survival.

1

REMEMBER, STRENGTH AIN'T EVERYTHING IN A MAN

"So Delilah said to Samson, 'Please tell me where your great strength lies, and with what you may be bound to afflict you.'" (Judges 16:6)

We honestly don't even know if Samson looked like a bodybuilder. We've been raised to think so because of the emphasis on his strength. The Bible says, "You shall conceive and bear a son. So then drink no wine or strong drink and eat nothing unclean, for the boy shall be a Nazarite to God from birth to the day of his death." (Judges 13:7) There's no mention of him gaining strength from working out or having bulging muscles. What does happen, though, in chapter 14:6, is that the Spirit of the Lord rushed on him, and he tore the lion apart barehanded, as one might tear apart a kid. It was the Spirit of the Lord that made him strong. It was the Spirit of the Lord upon him that caused him to do superhuman feats and wonders. We can't say for sure that Samson was this muscular, handsome man.

I bring this up because when you're looking to be in a relationship with a man, strength outside of God's will means nothing. Yes, he could rip a lion apart with his bare hands, but outside of that,

Samson had significant issues. He wasn't a great communicator; he had problems with women, was impulsive, and was unable to control his sexual desires. Sometimes we look at men ONLY when the Spirit of God is upon them and ignore when the Spirit of God is NOT with them.

Woman of God, it's possible for a man to be used by the Spirit of God but not filled with the Spirit of God. It's possible for a man to have moments of spirit-led strength but, outside of that, be a complete jerk. Women can testify to this. We know about the man who preached the glory of God but abused his mother at home. We know about the men who can slay people in the spirit but slay your emotions with empty words and promises. Be wise. Be sober. Be vigilant. Do not be afraid to overlook brothers who the Spirit uses in specific spaces but also abuse the Spirit by not tapping into it for their weaknesses and shortcomings. You don't have time for that. I promise you, Delilah knew this and leveraged his weaknesses against him. For us today, avoid the Samsons in the church altogether. Deal with men who are striving to be strong in the spirit all the time, by God's grace. Pray and ask God to discern between a man being used by the Spirit versus a man being filled and led by the Spirit.

"IT'S POSSIBLE FOR A MAN TO HAVE MOMENTS OF SPIRIT-LED STRENGTH BUT, OUTSIDE OF THAT, BE A COMPLETE JERK."

The Gem Being Dropped:

Don't fall for men who are only used by the Spirit of God, but choose not to let the Holy Spirit help them overcome significant issues that could affect you in a relationship.

2

AN INDEPENDENT WOMAN IS A PROBLEM IN PATRIARCHAL CIRCLES

"And the lords of the Philistines came up to her and said to her, 'Entice him, and find out where his great strength lies...'" (Judges 16:5)

"She considers a field and buys it; from her profits, she plants a vineyard. She girds herself with strength, and strengthens her arms." (Proverbs 31:16-17)

You will be maligned, misunderstood, and dragged when you're a woman who can make it on your own. Delilah was anything but weak. She had her own home, lived independently, and made strategic choices for her survival. She was not under the covering of a husband, nor was she under the control of a father or brother. When the Philistines approached her, they did so because they knew she had the power to act on her own terms.

But Delilah's story is not just about independence—it's about survival in a world that rarely made space for women to have autonomy. Dr. Wilda Gafney states, *"In the text, Delilah doesn't know that Samson's strength is a matter of religious observance. She is not intentionally setting herself against Samson or his god. She is a pragmatist trying to save her life because she knows that death follows in Samson's wake, at his hands and those of the Philistines."*

Samson was no innocent victim. He had a history of recklessness, playing games with women, using his strength as a weapon, and leaving destruction behind him. He was a warrior who had no problem killing for the sake of his ego. Delilah had seen what happened to the Philistine women before her. **His first Philistine wife was burned alive because of his impulsive choices**. So, if you were Delilah, would you take the risk of trusting him?

Women are often penalized for doing what they need to do to survive. Delilah is not celebrated for her independence because it doesn't fit the neat, moral conclusion that many want from her story. She is Philistine, not Israelite. She is a woman moving in a world that does not care about her well-being. And in patriarchal narratives, independent women—especially those outside the dominant culture—are rarely given the benefit of the doubt.

This same tension exists today, especially for Black women. One minute, we are praised for being strong, independent, educated, and self-sufficient. We are admired for building businesses, taking care of our families, and securing our own futures. But the moment we do not need a man to survive, we are told we are too much, too masculine, too independent to love. Society demands that we be resilient but punishes us when we don't shrink ourselves to accommodate fragile egos.

But independent women do not intimidate the right kind of men. A woman who has built a life for herself should not have to apologize for her strength. She should not have to make herself small to be chosen. What this means is that independent women must seek relationships with men who desire **partnership, not control.** Love should not require that you shrink your accomplishments, mute your voice, or pretend to be helpless just to be palatable.

To truly understand Delilah's choices—or those of women today—we must tell the whole story, not just the parts that make the storytellers look good. Context matters. And only by exploring the full narrative can we grasp the complexity of these decisions and the systems that shape them. And only by exploring the full narrative can we grasp the complexity of these decisions and the systems that shape them

> "TO TRULY UNDERSTAND DELILAH'S CHOICES OR THOSE OF WOMEN TODAY WE MUST TELL THE WHOLE STORY, NOT JUST THE PARTS THAT MAKE THE STORYTELLERS LOOK GOOD."

The Gem Being Dropped:

Independence attracts misunderstandings, but that's not your problem to fix. Stay true to who you are, and surround yourself with those who respect your full self. The right people will celebrate your strength, not resent it.

3

PLAYING THE PATRIARCHAL GAME DOESN'T MEAN YOU HAVE TO LOSE

"When Delilah saw that he had told her all his heart, she sent and called for the lords of the Philistines..."(-Judges 16:18)

"Wisdom is the principal thing; therefore get wisdom. And in all your getting, get understanding." (Proverbs 4:7)

Delilah came out of this situation looking like a boss babe—untouched, unharmed, and paid. But let's be clear: she wasn't simply playing a game for fun—she was navigating an impossible situation.

Samson was not just some love-drunk man smitten with Delilah. He was a warrior with a reputation for violence, a man who had slaughtered Philistines by the thousands and left destruction in his wake. He wasn't gentle, meek, or mild on Tinder—he was a force of war. And Delilah had to ask herself: What happens to me if I don't cooperate? If she refused the Philistines, would they kill her too? If she entertained Samson too long, would she put herself at risk?

Women throughout history have had to make impossible choices to survive in systems that were not designed for them to win. This does not mean we celebrate the system, but we recognize the reality of moving through it. In the words of Dr. Wilda Gafney, "Delilah is not punished for what she does to Samson." She does not repent. She does not suffer. She simply walks away from the story, free and financially secure. Unlike so many biblical women whose fates end in tragedy or subjugation, Delilah refuses to be the casualty of a man's war.

And let's be honest—society often treats women as keys, pawns, and disposable bodies used to unlock men's power. Some men will look at you as a stepping stone, a resource, or a challenge to conquer. They will test your loyalty without offering commitment, drain your energy without replenishing you, and try to strip you of power while using yours to get ahead. When you recognize that the game is rigged against you, wisdom says: **Don't let them play you.**

I'm speaking primarily to women in abusive, traumatic, or challenging situations. Survival is not betrayal. If you have to strategize, do it. If you have to protect yourself financially, do it. If you have to move in silence, do it. Being wise about your safety and well-being is not a sin—it is survival. Play the game so that you don't lose, but let the spirit lead you in how you move.

The Gem Being Dropped:

We live in a society that is not always fair to women. But don't let these jokers underestimate you, your wits, and your power. You are allowed to outsmart, outlive, and outshine the status quo. Do what you need to do to survive—and thrive.

4

LOVE SHOULDN'T FEEL LIKE A GAME

*"Then she said to him, 'How can you say, "I love you,"
when your heart is not with me?... And it came to pass,
when she pestered him daily with her words and pressed
him, so that his soul was vexed to death..." (Judges
16:15-16)*

*"There is no fear in love; but perfect love casts out fear,
because fear involves torment. But he who fears has not
been made perfect in love." (1 John 4:18)*

It's never stated that Delilah loved Samson. But the Bible does say that Samson loved Delilah. And yet, his version of love was a game—an obsessive push-and-pull that had nothing to do with real commitment.

Samson's "love" for Delilah looks less like devotion and more like infatuation—shallow, consuming, and ultimately self-destructive. He plays games with her, lying to her three times about the source of his strength. Meanwhile, Delilah tests and manipulates him, pressing him until he finally gives in. Their entire relationship is a toxic cycle where trust, transparency, and emotional safety are nowhere to be found.

How many women today find themselves in this same cycle? A man declares his love but makes her jump through hoops to prove hers. One day, he's all in; the next, he's distant and cold. He leaves her guessing, testing, doubting herself. That's not love. That's manipulation.

I've spoken to countless women who find themselves trapped in these dynamics—constantly questioning a man's intentions, overanalyzing his texts, or trying to decode his feelings through cryptic behavior. One woman shared how she spent months wondering if the man she was dating was serious about her. He would compliment her, make grand promises about the future, and then disappear for days without explanation. She said it felt like trying to solve a riddle with no answer. This emotional ambiguity left her exhausted and insecure, turning her into someone she didn't recognize—an anxious, hyper-vigilant version of herself, always searching for clues in his words and actions.

Love should feel like clarity, not confusion. Like security, not suspicion. Like a steady rhythm, not a riddle you can't solve. Love should never make you feel like you have to become a Delilah Detective just to pull out the truth from a man you're getting to know.

Samson played in Delilah's face three times. And yes, though their circumstances were different, the pattern is all too familiar. A man says he loves you—but his actions leave you exhausted, anxious, and questioning your worth. If you have to second-guess his words, if you're constantly being tested or asked to prove yourself, then what he's offering isn't love—it's a performance.

Samson's love was a games-played love, not agape love. True love communicates clearly, builds trust, and nurtures a sense of security. If you're in a relationship where you feel like you're constantly solving puzzles, trying to decode mixed signals, or proving your worth, ask yourself: Is this truly aligned with what God desires for me?

Love should feel engaging and exciting with forward momentum, not like you're trapped in an endless guessing game.

The Gem Being Dropped:

Stay away from relationships that feel like a game. You deserve love that's uncomplicated, direct, and dreamy. Love that calms your heart and makes you feel seen, cherished, and valued.

5

TELL YOUR OWN STORY AND OWN IT

> *"Afterward it happened that he loved a woman in the Valley of Sorek, whose name was Delilah." (Judges 16:4)*

Delilah's story has been used for centuries to demonize female sexuality and portray women as conniving temptresses. She has been preached to be a sex worker, whore, or promiscuous woman. However, an intentional reading of the story does not support this. At all.

"In the interpretative tradition, Delilah's character has been hypersexualized though it is Samson who sleeps his way through Israel and Philistia." – Dr. Wil Gafney

History is often written by those who want to paint themselves as victors instead of oppressors and perpetrators. And the person who honestly had issues with sexual ethics and reckless decisions was Samson, not Delilah. I bring this up because I want us, as Christian women, to start telling our side of the story.

Delilah isn't able to share her version of events, but today we can. She can't explicitly share her struggles, motivations, or life experiences that led her to choose to be part of Samson's demise.

But what's true—and isn't often spoken about—is how much of Samson's downfall was because of his own horrible choices and lack of self-control. He ended up at Delilah's house. He kept going to her house. He was the one who caused his own destruction. It was not her sexiness, allurement, or simply her being a woman that brought Samson down.

And let's not overlook a critical detail: Delilah never cut Samson's hair. That part of the story is almost always misrepresented. She lulled him to sleep, yes. She got the secret out of him, yes. But when it came to actually cutting his hair—the symbolic act that stripped him of his power— it was the men hiding in the inner room who did it (Judges 16:19). Delilah set the stage, but it was the men who finished the job.

How often are women blamed for things we did not do? How often are we cast as the villains while the real perpetrators slip away unseen? How often do we bear the weight of stories that were twisted to make men look like victims?

Think about the way rivers carve through rock over time. Nature shows us that water is often blamed for the erosion of mountains, but the truth is that the rock's inherent weaknesses—its fractures, its composition—are what allow the water to break it down. Samson's downfall wasn't Delilah—it was his own vulnerabilities, his refusal to address his weaknesses, and his insistence on placing himself in harm's way.

Too often, women are cast as the sole villains in stories where the downfall of a man is concerned. It's an ancient narrative, one that places undue blame on women while ignoring the man's agency, actions, and choices. From Eve to Jezebel to Delilah, women have been used as scapegoats for male failure. But Delilah's story challenges us to look deeper and to reclaim the narratives that have been written about us, especially the ones that distort our humanity.

I've had my share of being mischaracterized. I've been called names for speaking up, for taking a stand, for challenging harmful teachings. And like Delilah, I've been written into stories as the villain when all I did was exist unapologetically in spaces others found uncomfortable. But I've learned to tell my own story. To speak my truth. To correct the narratives that don't align with who I am.

Delilah teaches us that we don't have to be silent participants in stories written by others. We have the power to tell our side, to reclaim our experiences, and to shed light on the truth.

"THE PERSON WHO HONESTLY HAD ISSUES WITH SEXUAL ETHICS AND DECISIONS WAS SAMSON, NOT DELILAH."

The Gem Being Dropped:

You are the author of your own story. Refrain from letting others write it for you. Embrace your experiences, both good and bad, because they make you who you are. Challenge the limitations placed on you and rewrite any stories that hold you back. Speak your truth, even if it's messy or uncomfortable. Your voice matters.

TIME TO DROP YOUR OWN GEMS:

- Have you ever been drawn to someone whose spiritual strengths masked deeper flaws that affected you negatively? How can you develop the discernment to recognize a man who is led by God's Spirit consistently, rather than only in certain moments?

- What does it look like for you to claim your own narrative and rewrite stories that have been told about you?

- Consider a relationship or connection that felt like a game—a cycle of ambiguity, testing, or manipulation. How did it affect your peace, and what boundaries can you set to guard your heart against similar dynamics in the future?

  Delilah leveraged her position to ensure her survival and gain independence.

- Think about when you felt forced to make difficult choices to navigate a challenging environment. How did these choices impact you, and what wisdom or resilience did you gain?

- Have you ever felt like you had to use your charm or beauty to get ahead? How can we navigate situations strategically while staying true to ourselves?

- Delilah's story has often been twisted to fit a narrative that vilifies her. Reflect on areas where you may have been unfairly judged or misrepresented by others. How can you take control of these perceptions, either by sharing your truth or by moving forward without the need for others' approval?

- Imagine you could meet Delilah today. What would you want to tell her?

_____

_____

_____

_____

_____

_____

_____

_____

_____

_____

_____

_____

15

LESSONS FROM QUEEN VASHTI

Location: Queen Vashti lived in Persia, specifically in the royal palace at Susa, the capital of the Persian Empire, during the reign of King Xerxes (also known as Ahasuerus). (Esther 1:2, Esther 1:9, Esther 1:19)

RELATIONSHIP STATUS: DETHRONED & DISMISSED.

FAST FACTS:

◆ Vashti is known for her boldness and willingness to assert her dignity, refusing to appear before the king and his guests when he called her to display her beauty (Esther 1:10-12).

◆ Her decision to defy the king's command was highly controversial and led to her removal as queen, setting the stage for Esther to later become queen (Esther 1:19-21).

◆ Though only briefly mentioned in the Book of Esther, Vashti's story is often seen as an example of a woman standing up for her self-respect and boundaries, even in the face of severe consequences.

LIFE EVENTS:

♦ During a lavish banquet hosted by King Xerxes, Vashti was summoned to appear before him and his guests to show off her beauty, likely in a humiliating or objectifying manner (Esther 1:10-11).

♦ Vashti refused the king's command, an act that shocked the court and angered Xerxes, leading him to seek counsel on how to handle her defiance (Esther 1:12).

♦ At the advice of his advisors, Xerxes deposed Vashti to prevent other women in the kingdom from following her example of defiance (Esther 1:16-19).

♦ Vashti's removal opened the door for a new queen, leading to the search that ultimately brought Esther to the palace and into her role in saving the Jewish people (Esther 2:1-4).

THE WOMEN WHO CAN RELATE:

♦ Women who have set boundaries and upheld their dignity, even when it cost them a relationship, position, or societal approval.

♦ Women who have faced backlash for prioritizing self-respect and values over compliance or submission.

♦ Women who've been objectified or pressured to act in dehumanizing ways and bravely said "no" to protect their integrity.

♦ Women who have made difficult choices to protect their self-worth, even when it meant walking away from comfort or prestige.

- ◆ Women who have experienced the grief of losing something significant— whether a relationship, status, or job—because they stood up for their beliefs and emerged stronger.

- ◆ Women who resonate with the struggle of societal or relational expectations to "perform" or look a certain way but choose authenticity over conformity.

- ◆ Women who are trailblazers inspire others to value their worth, even if they don't immediately see the impact of their choices.

- ◆ Women who have been judged or criticized for asserting their boundaries yet remain committed to honoring their convictions.

- ◆ Women healing from the consequences of choosing self-worth over external validation, understanding their value is inherent.

- ◆ Women who feel called to embody "queen energy," standing confidently in their worth and refusing to be defined by anyone else's standards.

Sister, have you ever been at a party where things spiraled out of control? Maybe a work function turned into a tequila-fueled extravaganza or a family reunion devolved into drunken karaoke. That's the scene Queen Vashti walked into, according to the Book of Esther. Often dismissed as the disobedient wife, Vashti's story has much more to teach us about self-worth, boundaries, and staying true to ourselves.

It's ancient Persia, 480 BC, a patriarchal world where women were often treated as property. King Ahasuerus, drunk on power (and probably wine), throws a six-month party and demands Vashti parade her beauty before his equally drunk court. She's summoned like a trophy, her dignity ignored.

But Vashti wasn't just any queen. Her refusal to comply wasn't rebellion—it was a bold declaration of self-respect in a world that demanded submission. Let's unpack the gems her story has for us modern-day queens.

YOU DON'T OWE A MAN ANYTHING, ESPECIALLY YOUR BODY

"On the seventh day, when the heart of the king was merry with wine, he commanded... to bring Queen Vashti before the king, wearing her royal crown, in order to show her beauty to the people and the officials, for she was beautiful to behold. But Queen Vashti refused to come at the king's command... therefore the king was furious, and his anger burned within him." (Esther 1:10-12)

The Bible tells us, very clearly and concisely, that "Queen Vashti refused to come" (Esther 1:12). That's right, she said no. No to being paraded around like a trophy wife. No to having her dignity diminished for the amusement of a bunch of inebriated men.

Vashti understood something crucial: she didn't owe the king, or any man for that matter, her body or her self-worth. She wasn't an object to be displayed but a woman with agency and the right to say no.

"QUEEN VASHTI REMINDS US THAT YOUR 'NO' MATTERS."

This resonates deeply, doesn't it? In our world, societal pressures and unrealistic beauty standards can make us feel like we owe men something—a certain look, a certain level of submissiveness, or even worse, physical intimacy when we're not comfortable. But Vashti reminds us that our bodies are our own temples. We have the right to set boundaries and refuse anything that feels like a violation of our self-respect.

Saying no can be scary, honey. It might lead to arguments, disappointment, or even rejection. But just like Vashti, claiming your autonomy is the foundation of a healthy relationship—one built on mutual respect and genuine connection.

It's also important to note that Queen Vashti said no to her husband. In many cultures, it's expected that wives are not allowed to turn down requests for sex from their husbands. It's considered improper to go against what your husband requests. Queen Vashti reminds us that your "no" matters. You're allowed to honor your desire not to do something if it makes you feel uncomfortable, unsafe, or undesirable. Do not be afraid to say no. Do not be afraid to honor the discomfort your body is feeling.

The Gem Being Dropped:

Your "no" matters always. Never feel like your desire to not do something should be suppressed or ignored. Honor your boundaries

and never feel obligated to give away any part of yourself that doesn't
align with your dignity.

2

KNOW WHEN TO WALK AWAY

"Wisdom is the principal thing; therefore get wisdom. And in all your getting, get understanding." (Proverbs 4:7)

Let me tell you about the little boy who got his hand stuck in a vase. He'd reached in to grab a small toy at the bottom, but he couldn't pull his hand back out once his fingers wrapped around it. His parents tried everything—soap, water, even a little butter—but his hand stayed stuck. Finally, someone asked, "What's in your hand?" He opened his fist and out fell the toy. With his hand free, the vase slid right off. The moral? Sometimes, the only way to free yourself is to let go.

That story reminds me of Vashti. When her dignity was on the line, she chose to let go of her crown and walk away from her role as queen. It wasn't an easy decision. The crown came with power, prestige, and privilege, but it also came with conditions that crossed her boundaries. Her refusal wasn't just about saying no to King Ahasuerus—it was about saying yes to herself.

As women, we've all been conditioned at some point to hold on to things that validate our worth in the eyes of others. A title, a relationship, a position, or even a reputation can feel too valuable to let go of, no matter how much it costs us. But wisdom is knowing when to walk away.

Vashti shows us that letting go isn't a loss—it's liberation. It's choosing self-respect over societal expectations. It's trusting yourself enough to release what no longer aligns with your spirit. And yes, stepping into the unknown is scary, but freedom is worth the risk.

The Gem Being Dropped

Wisdom is knowing when to stay and when to leave. Trust yourself enough to walk away when your dignity is at stake.

3

IT'S OKAY TO GRIEVE WHAT COMES WITH SAYING NO

"If it pleases the king, let a royal decree go out from him, and let it be recorded in the laws of the Persians and the Medes, so that it will not be altered, that Vashti shall come no more before King Ahasuerus; and let the king give her royal position to another who is better than she."
(Esther 1:19)

Okay, Vashti said no. But King Ahasuerus, in his drunken stupor, wasn't exactly thrilled. Sensing a power play, his advisors fanned the flames further, convincing him that Vashti's disobedience threatened his authority. Long story short, Vashti gets banished from the palace and stripped of her queenly title.

This part of the story can be tough to swallow. Vashti stood her ground, yet she suffered the consequences. It's a reminder that saying no doesn't always come with a happily ever after. There might be pain, loss, and a period of grieving what you've had to give up.

Vashti's grief doesn't diminish the power of her decision. She chose her integrity over the comfort of being a queen. She prioritized her self-respect, even when it meant losing her position.

This speaks volumes to us in our relationships. Sometimes,

setting boundaries and saying no means walking away from situations or relationships that don't align with our values. It can be heartbreaking, but ultimately, it allows us to create space for healthier connections and a life that feels authentic.

Imagine Rosa Parks saying no to giving up her seat on that bus. Her "no" came with immense consequences—arrest, public scrutiny, and the weight of igniting a civil rights movement. But her no wasn't about ease or convenience; it was about standing firm in what she believed was right. Vashti's no mirrors this courage. Like Rosa Parks, Vashti knew that her no would cause discomfort, but she also knew that her dignity mattered more than avoiding the fallout.

And just like in nature, pruning—a process where dead or overgrown branches are cut away—can look harsh and even feel like loss. But without pruning, a tree can't grow to its fullest potential. Saying no and grieving what comes with it is a form of pruning. It's painful, but it clears space for growth, health, and new possibilities.

If your "no" brings grief, heartbreak, or disappointment, it's okay to sit with those emotions and feel them deeply. Grieving is not a sign of weakness; it's a recognition of the cost of staying true to yourself. Honor those feelings while holding onto the truth that your integrity is worth every tear.

The Gem Being Dropped:

Sometimes, saying no comes with loss. Grieving is part of valuing your integrity. Embrace the pain, knowing it's a pathway to truer, healthier connections.

4

YOU'RE STILL A QUEEN
WITHOUT A KING

"You shall also be a crown of glory in the hand of the Lord, and a royal diadem in the hand of your God."
(Isaiah 62:3)

Vashti reminds us that queen behavior is not contingent on a man calling you a queen, but it's deeply rooted in your mindset, actions, and the way you carry yourself. Your power as a woman is not connected to having a king by your side, but it flows from how you see yourself and the confidence you exude. It's about knowing your worth, regardless of who acknowledges it.

Think about a peanut butter and jelly sandwich. Peanut butter and jelly together is a culinary marriage made in heaven—two flavors that perfectly complement each other. But understand this: peanut butter is still peanut butter without the jelly, and jelly is still jelly without the peanut butter. They don't lose their identity or their essence just because they're not paired together. And it's the same with us as queens. Whether you have a king or not, you're still a queen in your own right, complete and whole, lacking nothing.

Vashti, despite losing her crown, never lost her dignity, her self-respect, or her power. She didn't need a title to validate her worth because she knew that her value wasn't tied to a crown or a throne. She stood firm in her convictions, even when it cost her everything because she understood that true power comes from within. Vashti teaches us that our worth isn't dependent on our relationship status, our proximity to power, or external validation. We are queens simply because we exist because God has created us with inherent value and purpose.

So, even if you're navigating life without a king by your side, know that you are still regal, still powerful, and still deserving of love and respect. Your singleness or your independence doesn't diminish your queendom. In fact, it's often in those seasons of solitude that you discover just how strong and capable you truly are. Embrace your identity as a queen—because a true queen doesn't need a king to shine; she radiates from within.

"A TRUE QUEEN DOESN'T NEED A KING TO SHINE; SHE RADIATES FROM WITHIN."

The Gem Being Dropped:

Your worth is intrinsic; it's not tied to anyone else. You are a queen because you embody dignity, strength, and purpose.

5

REDEFINING OBEDIENCE: GOD OVER MAN

"But Peter and the other apostles answered and said: 'We ought to obey God rather than men.'" (Acts 5:29)

Imagine a musician in a large orchestra. The conductor waves their baton, directing the musicians to play in harmony. But one violinist hears something off—a discord in the music. They realize the conductor's tempo has slipped, leading the entire orchestra astray. What should the violinist do? Keep playing along to avoid disrupting the performance, or trust the sheet music and play according to the original score?

Now picture Vashti. She was in a position where everyone expected her to "play along." When the king demanded she parade herself like a trophy, the world said, "Obey your husband." But Vashti knew something wasn't right. Her refusal wasn't just disobedience to her husband; it was an act of obedience to a higher calling—honoring her dignity and God's design for her life.

True obedience isn't about blind submission to human authority. It's about aligning with God's truth, even when it means going against the expectations of others.

Vashti's story reminds us that obeying God may require saying "no" to worldly demands, even when the cost is high.

As women, we face countless pressures to conform—to meet cultural expectations, to keep the peace, and to prioritize others over ourselves. But Vashti challenges us to prioritize divine convictions over societal norms. She teaches us that real obedience isn't about pleasing people; it's about living in alignment with God's purpose for our lives.

The Gem Being Dropped:

Obedience isn't blind submission; it's aligning with God's truth over the world's demands. Like Vashti, trust the God - orchestrated score and play in tune with your higher calling.

TIME TO DROP YOUR OWN GEMS:

♦ Have you ever had to set a boundary that led to loss or heartache? How did you grieve that loss, and what did you learn about yourself in the process?

♦ What does "owning your autonomy" mean to you? Are there any specific areas in your relationships where you feel called to reclaim your voice or set clearer boundaries?

♦ Queen Vashti's story reminds us that worth isn't tied to titles, relationships, or external validation. Where do you feel most challenged to believe in your own worth? How can you remind yourself of your intrinsic value, especially when external voices tell you otherwise?

♦ Think about a time when you stayed in a situation that didn't align with your values or integrity. What kept you there, and what would it take for you to walk away from similar situations in the future with confidence?

♦ In a world that often values compliance over conviction, how can you cultivate a sense of inner strength that empowers you to honor your boundaries, even when it's uncomfortable or unpopular?

◆ Reflect on moments when you've placed obedience to God's purpose above others' expectations or demands. What internal struggles did you face, and how did it feel to choose God's truth over worldly pressures?

◆ Reflect on what it means to be a "queen" without needing a king. How can you embrace your identity, strength, and purpose independent of anyone else's validation or acknowledgment?

16

LESSONS
FROM
ESTHER

*Location: The Persian empire in the royal palace in Susa, a major city and capital of Elam
(Esther 1:2; Esther 2:8)*

RELATIONSHIP STATUS: THE KING'S FAVORITE WIFE

FAST FACTS:

- Esther's Hebrew name is Hadassah, which means "myrtle." (Esther 2:7)
- She used her Persian name while living in the palace. (Esther 2:7)
- She was an orphan raised by her cousin Mordecai. (Esther 2:7)
- The feast of Purim was established to commemorate the bravery of Esther and the fact that the Jewish people were saved from extermination and genocide. (Esther 9:20-22)

LIFE EVENTS:

- Chosen to be queen after King Xerxes deposed Queen Vashti (Esther 2:17)
- She risked her life by approaching the king uninvited, a crime punishable by death unless the king extended his scepter (Esther 4:11; Esther 5:1-2)
- She hosted two banquets where she revealed Haman's plot to annihilate the Jews. (Esther 7:1-6)
- Saved her people (Esther 8:5-8; Esther 9:1)

THE WOMEN WHO CAN RELATE:

- Women who've been placed in influential positions that require immense courage and wisdom to navigate.
- Women who've walked into unexpected opportunities that led them to greatness, despite humble or difficult beginnings.
- Women who are passionate about saving others and advocating courageously for their people or loved ones.
- Women who've had to make life-changing decisions, balancing personal risk with the greater good.
- Women who've been forced to make the best of horrible situations, rising above their circumstances with resilience.
- Women who are aware of their "pretty privilege" and use it strategically and wisely for a greater purpose.

◆ Women caught between two worlds, navigating cultural or social challenges while staying true to themselves.

◆ Women who have been in relationships with men who had other women

◆ Women who have been exploited for the sake of a man's desires and wants

Esther is often seen through the lens of a Cinderella or fairytale—an orphaned girl becomes queen. But this story is not a Disney movie. It is about a bold sister navigating a ruthless political landscape, using her intelligence and, yes, even her beauty, to save her people. Her life offers lessons on faith, sex, and relationships that resonate with us strong, modern-day women.

1

IT WASN'T A BEAUTY PAGEANT. IT WAS A SEX RING. AND IT WASN'T OKAY.

"Then the king's servants who attended him said, 'Let beautiful young virgins be sought for the king; and let the king appoint officers in all the provinces of his kingdom, that they may gather all the beautiful young virgins to Shushan the citadel, into the women's quarters, under the custody of Hegai the king's eunuch, custodian of the women. And let beauty preparations be given them." (Esther 2:2-3)

"Each young woman's turn came to go into King Ahasuerus after she had completed twelve months' preparation, according to the regulations for the women, for thus were the days of their preparation apportioned: six months with oil of myrrh, and six months with perfumes and preparations for beautifying women."
(Esther 2:12)

> *"Defend the poor and fatherless; do justice to the afflict-*
> *ed and needy. Deliver the poor and needy; free them*
> *from the hand of the wicked." (Psalm 82:3-4)*

"YES, WE NEED MORE ESTHERS, BUT WE ALSO DON'T NEED ANY MORE SITUATIONS OR ENVIRONMENTS THAT CALL FOR AN ESTHER, EITHER."

I'll never forget when I watched the television series, "Roots" and absorbed the scene where the African American people were being auctioned off. They were treated like animals, being sold for their bodies, strength, and minds to be used in horrific ways in the name of capitalism. The auction block has long been a horrible sight. And when I think about Esther, I don't think about stages; I think about auctions. Let's allow things to be first: We must dismantle the myth that Esther's journey to becoming queen was some glamorous selection process. Sis, that "beauty contest" was a royal cattle call, similar to our brothers and sisters being auctioned off. It's often not viewed that way because...it was women. And somehow, in society, we've allowed that to be okay.

Young women were paraded in front of the king, objectified, and expected to be available for his pleasure. This wasn't a celebration of female beauty; it was a system that exploited women's bodies for male gratification. Studies on historical harems suggest a focus on acquiring women for the king's pleasure, with little to no agency for the women involved. Young women, often taken from conquered nations, were presented to the king not for competition but for a forced selection. This wasn't a celebration of female empowerment but a system of control. Still, even in our time, the trafficking and exploitation of women is a gross instance of injustice, and that system must be destroyed.

The International Labour Organization (ILO) estimates that 4.8 million people are currently in forced sexual exploitation, with women and girls making up 72% of victims. Thankfully, there are organizations like The Polaris Project and La Strada International that are rescuing victims and dismantling trafficking rings. It reminds me of Esther, who, although she was living in a horrid time when women lacked agency, chose to risk her life to advocate for her people.

On the flip side of that same coin, we cannot become so desensitized and demoralized to the use of sexual trafficking to the point that we celebrate the strength of victims more than putting more energy into the dismantling of these rings and the beliefs that support them in the first place. Yes, we need more Esthers, but we also don't need any more situations or environments that call for an Esther, either. Both need to be eradicated.

The Gem Being Dropped:

We must intentionally focus on eradicating exploitative systems rather than romanticizing the resilience of victims. Women are queens to be treasured, not prizes to be trafficked.

2

REMEMBER TO LEVERAGE YOUR GIFTS WITHOUT SELLING YOUR SOUL

"Now when the turn came for Esther the daughter of Abihail the uncle of Mordecai, who had taken her as his daughter, to go into the king, she requested nothing but what Hegai the king's eunuch, the custodian of the women, advised. And Esther obtained favor in the sight of all who saw her... The king loved Esther more than all the other women, and she obtained grace and favor in his sight more than all the virgins; so he set the royal crown upon her head and made her queen instead of Vashti."
(Esther 2:15-17)

"Let not mercy and truth forsake you; bind them around your neck, write them on the tablet of your heart, and so find favor and high esteem in the sight of God and man." (Proverbs 3:3-4)

"Charm is deceitful and beauty is passing, but a woman who fears the LORD, she shall be praised." (Proverbs 31:30)

Esther's story shows us the delicate balance between using our God-given gifts and standing firm in our values. Yes, she was beautiful. Yes, she was alluring. The book describes Esther finding favor with the king (Esther 2:17), but this doesn't imply manipulative seduction. Esther likely possessed a natural charm and wisdom that resonated with the king.

Furthermore, Esther understood the system she was in. She knew her beauty and charm were assets, tools she could use to navigate the power dynamics of the court. She played the game, but she didn't become a pawn.

Woman of God, we can learn from Esther. We live in a society that suggests we tone down our femininity. There's this expectation that a woman is expected to act like a man in a man's world. Where being more masculine means being more productive and getting the job done, and if we embrace our girliness or femininity too much, we will miss out on success. But Esther navigated her world by owning her gifts without compromising her integrity. She leaned into her God-given beauty and charm, yes, but with wisdom and strategy, never allowing the system to define her worth.

Esther was smart enough to understand the system she was placed in. She respected Hegai's advice and took what he recommended, trusting the insights of someone who understood the palace. And that's where her power shines. Esther didn't let her beauty become a bargaining chip; she saw it as one of many strengths, used strategically to fulfill a purpose. This wasn't desperation or a ploy—it was a divinely inspired use of the gifts God gave her without letting her identity get lost in the process.

Ladies, the world will constantly try to define what is "acceptable" femininity. We look at social media and see images of women who use their femininity in manipulative ways. We're bombarded with photos from the porn industry that distort feminine sexuality. If we want to be taken seriously, we run in the opposite direction.

Many women move away from their feminine essence because it doesn't seem to be the path to being a truly respected woman, listened to, and seen as powerful. But Esther's story shows us the truth: that power lies not in downplaying who we are but in fully stepping into our God-given gifts, beauty included, with wisdom.

Esther teaches us to embrace God's gifts, including our beauty, sensuality, and natural charisma. But she also shows us the importance of staying grounded, of knowing who we are beyond our outer appearance. This isn't about manipulation or desperation. It's about understanding that our gifts can be leveraged to fulfill a greater purpose without losing ourselves in the process.

The Gem Being Dropped:

It's okay to own your beauty and sensuality, sis. It's okay to tap into your beauty as an asset and necessity to get things done to the glory of God. These are gifts from God! But there's a crucial difference between owning your power and letting someone else control you. Use your gifts strategically, not desperately.

3

EMPLOY AGENCY IN A SYSTEM THAT WANTS TO USE YOUR BODY

"Go, gather all the Jews who are present in Shushan, and fast for me; neither eat nor drink for three days, night or day. My maids and I will fast likewise. And so I will go to the king, which is against the law, and if I perish, I perish!" (Esther 4:16)

"The LORD is my light and my salvation; whom shall I fear? The LORD is the strength of my life; of whom shall I be afraid?" (Psalm 27:1)

"Commit your works to the LORD, and your thoughts will be established." (Proverbs 16:3)

Esther's story is a sobering demonstration of rape culture. Remember, Mordecai warned her against going to the king uninvited, a sign that this wasn't always a consensual situation. It would appear that sometimes Esther had to service the king against her wishes. But Esther, with fierce courage, stepped outside the rules to save her people. She went to the king without his permission. She used her newfound position as queen to influence the king, ultimately saving the Jews from annihilation. Again, I love that Esther reminds us that women weren't as docile and well-behaved within the structures of their society.

It's like toddlers journeying through their alleged terrible twos. I prefer to call it their independent twos. They're learning the value of their agency. They're learning the power of yes and no. They're learning how to stand up for themselves. I would rather have an ounce of unbothered autonomy and agency of a toddler than resign myself to minimizing my needs just to be accepted. Esther leaves this for us to follow and adapt to our situations. She's like a toddler who defiantly steps to the King despite the possible consequences to save herself and her people. I remember the phrase, "better to ask forgiveness than permission." I believe that's what's happening here. Esther is teaching us that in a system that doesn't always value and respect you, stepping outside of what's accepted and expected is okay if it means standing up for yourself. Ask for forgiveness later if needed.

"EVEN IN A MESSED-UP SYSTEM, YOU HAVE AGENCY!"

The Gem Being Dropped:

Even in a messed-up system, you have agency. You can find creative ways to use the rules to your advantage and to advocate for yourself and your community. Don't be afraid to break the mold, sis, but do it with a plan.

4

SOMETIMES YOU HAVE TO HIDE YOURSELF TO SAVE YOURSELF

"Esther had not revealed her people or family, for Mordecai had charged her not to reveal it." (Esther 2:10)

"And Mordecai told them to answer Esther: 'Do not think in your heart that you will escape in the king's palace any more than all the other Jews. For if you remain completely silent at this time, relief and deliverance will arise for the Jews from another place, but you and your father's house will perish. Yet who knows whether you have come to the kingdom for such a time as this?'" (Esther 4:13-14)

"Behold, I send you out as sheep in the midst of wolves. Therefore be wise as serpents and harmless as doves." (Matthew 10:16)

Now, some might judge Esther because she wasn't some perfect saint. From a religious perspective, she concealed her identity and ethnicity. Her cousin Mordecai advised her to keep her heritage a secret when she became Queen of Persia. Only when it became necessary to reveal who she was to intercede with the King on behalf of her people did she disclose that she was Jewish. She hid her identity out of fear of persecution. And for many of us women today, unfortunately, there are still instances where it's wise to conceal who you are to protect who you are. Esther is here to remind us that you are worthy of love and that we understand why you do what you do.

For example, maybe you're in the thick of online dating. Because the online dating world can be a breeding ground for harassment and dangerous situations, you may protect yourself from unwanted advances by using a pseudonym and a different phone number, only revealing your real name after you've gotten to know someone.

In Esther's time, women weren't always seen as capable rulers. Likewise, there are women today who face gender bias in certain professions. It's not unlikely for a woman to downplay her accomplishments or avoid revealing her gender in online professional circles to avoid being overlooked. Esther wants to say that she sees you.

Financial security can also be a concern. You might hesitate to disclose your financial situation to a new partner, especially if you know you're the primary earner, fearing expectations or manipulation. Esther is here to say she gets it. It is completely understandable and expected.

Maybe you're someone who has mental health issues—or other physical illnesses. Mental health is still a topic steeped in stigma. It's completely human and understandable to exercise restraint and choose not to reveal a mental health condition for fear of judgment or being seen as less desirable until you feel comfortable and safe. And most women have experienced some level of trauma or abuse. Esther's situation involved a potential threat to her life. Similarly, a woman who has experienced stalking or abuse might choose not to reveal her details or location out of fear for her safety.

Esther's story is a gift for everyone who has felt the pressure to open up every part of ourselves before we're ready. She shows us that protecting your heart, your identity, and your life's details doesn't mean you're hiding; it means you're being discerning. Every relationship and setting doesn't deserve full access to the most sacred parts of you.

In Esther's final act of bravery, when she reveals her heritage to save her people, she demonstrates that there is a time for wisdom and courage. Both have their place. Her example invites us to hold space for our needs and boundaries while remaining open to moments that call us to rise and show up fully.

The Gem Being Dropped:

Discernment is your friend and ally. You can use wisdom and keep elements of your identity and personal information close to your chest until you're ready to reveal what is necessary for a relationship. Let go of guilt for protecting yourself and remember: true empowerment lies in knowing when to speak up and when to hold your peace. You are not weak for choosing to protect your heart and life—you're wise, just like Esther.

TIME TO DROP YOUR OWN GEMS:

- How does Esther's story challenge traditional views of women's roles in society and the church?

- How can we embrace our femininity and God-given gifts without falling into the trap of objectification?

- Have you ever felt like you had to "play the game" to get ahead? How can we navigate these situations with integrity?

- Have you ever felt pressured to leverage your sexuality in an unhealthy way? What did you do? What advice would you give to another woman facing a similar situation?

- What are your God-given gifts and talents? How can you use them to make a positive impact in your life and the lives of others?

- Do you struggle with shame or guilt around your past? How can you embrace God's forgiveness and move forward?

- How can we recognize and challenge systems that perpetuate a culture of rape or sexual exploitation?

17

LESSONS FROM QUEEN OF SHEBA

Location: The Queen of Sheba likely came from the Kingdom of Sheba, often associated with the region of modern-day Yemen or Ethiopia in ancient times (1 Kings 10:1; 2 Chronicles 9:1).

RELATIONSHIP STATUS: SINGLE & UNBOTHERED

FAST FACTS:

♦ The Queen of Sheba is known for her wisdom and curiosity; she traveled a great distance to test Solomon's wisdom and learn from him (1 Kings 10:1-2).

♦ She brought lavish gifts for Solomon, including gold, spices, and precious stones, and is remembered for her generosity (1 Kings 10:10).

♦ Her visit to Solomon established a mutual respect and admiration between the two rulers, bridging cultures and nations (1 Kings 10:13).

♦ Her journey highlights the fame of Solomon's wisdom and the international reach of his reputation at the time.

♦ Her name isn't Sheba; that's the name of her kingdom.

LIFE EVENTS:

- The Queen of Sheba heard of Solomon's wisdom and undertook a long journey with a large entourage to test him with difficult questions (1 Kings 10:1-2).
- She was so impressed by his wisdom, the splendor of his palace, court, and worship of God that she acknowledged the greatness of Solomon's God (1 Kings 10:4-9).
- She exchanged gifts and wealth with Solomon, and after a time, she returned to her own country, inspired and changed by her experience (1 Kings 10:10, 13).

THE WOMEN WHO CAN RELATE:

- Women who balance leadership, ambition, and femininity with grace, navigating spaces often dominated by men.
- Women who dare to leave their comfort zones and explore new territories or cultures to expand their horizons.
- Women who actively seek intellectual, spiritual, and emotional growth by pursuing mentors, knowledge, and wisdom across boundaries.
- Women who use their influence to form alliances, build bridges, and share resources, creating connections across diverse groups.
- Women who value meaningful relationships, holding out for

intellectual, spiritual, and emotional depth over surface-level connections.

♦ Women who set high standards in dating and relationships, demanding respect, admiration, and partnership on their terms.

♦ Women who ask questions boldly, seek answers unapologetically and pursue knowledge with curiosity and confidence.

♦ Women who invest thoughtfully in people and relationships, giving generously without compromising their self-worth or boundaries.

♦ Women who want to be seen and respected for their whole selves—beyond physical appearance or societal expectations.

♦ Women who are unapologetically themselves, embracing their femininity as a source of strength and influence.

The Queen of Sheba was a powerhouse long before Beyoncé asked, "Who runs the world?" She ruled with authority, intelligence, and grace at a time when women were expected to remain quiet and in the background. While the Bible gives us only a glimpse of her story, her life speaks volumes about owning one's worth, embracing one's sensuality, and rewriting the rules.

Often misunderstood as just a mysterious foreigner who visited Solomon, Sheba was much more—a monarch in her own right, ruling a wealthy and powerful kingdom. She defied the patriarchal system, shattering expectations and carving her path to success.

Her story isn't just about power; it's about knowing your value, using your voice, and refusing to let societal limits define you. What can this ancient queen teach us about ruling our own lives today?

1

EVALUATE THE PEOPLE YOU'RE INVESTING IN

"Now when the queen of Sheba heard of the fame of Solomon concerning the name of the Lord, she came to test him with hard questions."(1 Kings 10:1)

So, the real reason the Queen of Sheba's story has legs is her legendary visit to King Solomon. Now, the Bible keeps things pretty vague about the nature of their encounter. Some folks jump to wild conclusions, picturing some scandalous affair. But there's a much more empowering way to interpret this story. The Queen of Sheba wasn't some naive teenager falling for a pretty face. She was an intelligent ruler, likely older and more experienced than Solomon. So why would she travel a great distance just to... well, you know? Scholars suggest the Queen, having heard of Solomon's wisdom and impressive kingdom, embarked on a diplomatic mission. She wanted to see this famed ruler for herself, assess his capabilities, and potentially forge an alliance between their nations.

The Queen of Sheba teaches us a powerful lesson: only invest in men who bring their A-game. Before you get swept away by a sweet smile or a charming personality, take a step back and evaluate.

Remember, intimacy isn't just physical. It's also about mental and emotional connection. Hold out for someone who stimulates you on all levels, not just the bedroom kind. Is this guy someone who respects your goals? Does he challenge you intellectually? Does he inspire you to be your best self? Do you even like him? How do you genuinely feel when you're with him?

Think of yourself as a queen, sis. You deserve a partner who recognizes your worth and complements your journey. Just like the Queen of Sheba wouldn't have wasted her time on a man who didn't meet her standards, neither should you.

The Gem Being Dropped

Be bold and set high standards, sis! You are a worthy woman who deserves a man who elevates you, not diminishes you. Choose wisely, and don't be afraid to walk away from situations that don't serve your highest good.

2

GIVE WHAT YOU WON'T REGRET GIVING AWAY IN A RELATIONSHIP – BE STRATEGIC, NOT A DOORMAT

"Then she gave the king one hundred and twenty talents of gold, spices in great abundance, and precious stones. There never again came such abundance of spices as the queen of Sheba gave to King Solomon." (1 Kings 10:10)

I used to be a woman who felt like I had to perform and earn the accolades and attention of a man. I would give beyond my capacity and desire because, if I went above and beyond, he would see me, choose me, and love me. This never worked. Now, my relationship with giving has shifted significantly because, no matter what, relationships are a two-way street. You give, they give, right? Well, the Queen of Sheba provides us with a masterclass in giving strategically.

The Bible tells us she brought Solomon an extravagant amount of gold, spices, and precious stones. Some might see this as mere flattery, a way to please the king. But there's more to it than that.

These gifts were valuable resources from her kingdom. By

offering them, the Queen wasn't just showering Solomon with riches; she was establishing a trade relationship that would benefit both nations.

Think about it this way: In any relationship, healthy giving is about investing in the future. Healthy giving is about investing in a way that benefits you. Whether it's your time, energy, or emotional support, in a dating relationship, you want to give to someone from a place that honors your values, boundaries and desires with a suitor who reciprocates. In marriage, there are still boundaries, but there is room for more sacrificial giving because there's a covenant involved. But when evaluating a man for a long-term relationship—like the Queen of Sheba was doing with Solomon—give generously within your capacity.

The famous dating coach Samone Blakely, aka TorahCents, says, "Give in a way that you won't regret it if he ghosts you the next day." If you know deep down that if you cooked him that meal or bought him those shoes and you NEVER heard from him again, you would be as salty as ever, then evaluate why you're giving that to him. In dating, you only want to give from a place of who you are, not from a place of possible regret and disappointment. Giving strategically doesn't mean being a doormat. Don't be afraid to set boundaries and walk away from situations where your generosity is taken for granted. You deserve respect and reciprocity in all your relationships.

The Queen of Sheba wasn't some pushover. Her gifts weren't one-sided. The Bible mentions Solomon answering all her questions and showering her with gifts in return. The Queen gave strategically, ensuring her investment would yield a return. And it's the same for us. Be a giver, yes. But be a giver in a way that won't set yourself up for severe regret if the relationship doesn't work out. Sometimes disappointment is inevitable, but there are things we can do to protect and guard our giving hearts.

The Gem Being Dropped:

Don't be afraid to give generously in your relationships but give with intention. Invest in people who appreciate you and contribute positively to your life. Remember, true partnership is about mutual support and growth.

3

EMBRACE THE HIGHEST VERSION OF YOURSELF

"She came to Jerusalem with a very great retinue..." (1 Kings 10:2)

The Queen of Sheba embodied this kind of self-assuredness to the max. I imagine she had that inner glow, that fierce confidence that makes you a force to be reckoned with. The Bible describes her arrival at Solomon's court as a grand spectacle. Imagine a powerful queen, her crown a beaming halo against the desert sun, adorned in jewels that winked like constellations in the midday sun. Her exquisite garments were shimmering silks that flowed in the desert breeze. She was leading a massive caravan stretching as far as the eye could see, overflowing with treasures that gleamed like promises of untold riches. This queen wasn't shrinking back, hiding her amazing aura. She owned her power and commanded respect with every step.

The Queen of Sheba teaches us a vital lesson: embrace the highest version of yourself. Embracing the highest version of yourself means not shying away from whatever you need to foster personal and spiritual growth. It means unapologetically removing people, situations, and mindsets that don't serve your goals, positive habits, and purpose. Yes, there will be doubts. Yes, there will be pressure from the church, family, society, and people who are accustomed to the unhealthy, broken version of you. But don't dim your light to fit in with anyone or anything. Own your talents, intelligence, and unique beauty—all of it! Think of yourself as a queen ruling over your kingdom. You have something valuable to offer the world, and it's time to share your gifts confidently. Don't be afraid to enter the spotlight and let your brilliance shine.

"CONFIDENCE IS THE ULTIMATE ACCESSORY, SIS!"

The Gem Being Dropped:

Confidence is the ultimate accessory, sis. Work on self-love, celebrate your strengths and don't be afraid to show the world who you are. When you embrace your highest self, you attract the kind of love and respect you deserve.

4

EMPLOY YOUR FEMININITY
IN THE WORKPLACE

> *"...There never again came such abundance of spices as the queen of Sheba gave to King Solomon." (1 Kings 10:10)*

The Queen of Sheba wasn't just a ruler; she was a savvy businesswoman. The Bible mentions her kingdom being renowned for its wealth and trade. She understood the power of economics and used her feminine wiles to her advantage. Some folks think femininity and power are at odds. There's this expectation that a woman must act like a man in a man's world. Being more masculine means being more productive and getting the job done. If we embrace our girliness or femininity too much, we'll miss out on success. But I feel less stressed and more alive when I'm in tune with my true self.

We were taught that feminine means weak. Have you ever judged a feminine woman as weak, superficial, or ditzy? We've convinced ourselves that we have to be fully in our masculinity to match it with men. But it's artificial. It doesn't mean you won't use your masculine qualities to get things done, but you'll balance this with your grounded, attractive feminine essence. At first, it might feel weird—like it's not safe to be feminine.

Many women have linked their womanhood with being hurt, betrayed, or controlled. So many women feel uncomfortable with unwanted attention from men, even if it's a harmless stare. Or maybe you were told not to be too girly or too sexy. But I'm learning to embrace my sexiness as a preacher without being taken advantage of. Keep solid and healthy boundaries without dimming your radiance. It's politically incorrect to be too feminine. No one will tell you that you need to act like a man, but I think I did to adapt. We look at social media and see images of women who use their femininity in manipulative ways, or the porn industry has distorted feminine sexuality.

When we see these images, we feel like if we want to be taken seriously, we must run in the opposite direction. Many women move away from their feminine essence because it doesn't seem to be the path to being genuinely respected, listened to, and seen as powerful. But I'm learning I can be both powerful and feminine.

The Queen of Sheba teaches women to be strong, intelligent leaders while embracing their femininity.

Femininity encompasses grace, intuition, empathy, and even a touch of charm. These qualities can be powerful tools in the workplace. Use your intuition to navigate difficult situations, your empathy to build strong relationships with colleagues, and your grace to handle pressure with poise.

The Queen of Sheba likely used her diplomatic skills and cultural savvy to secure trade deals with other nations. She understood that collaboration and building relationships were crucial to success. There's a difference between being assertive and being aggressive. Channel your inner Queen of Sheba and use your femininity to influence and inspire, not dominate and belittle.

The Gem Being Dropped:

Embrace your femininity, honey! It's not a weakness; it's a strength. Use your unique skills and strengths to navigate the workplace and achieve your goals.

5

USE YOUR VOICE AND AUTHORITY TO GET WHAT YOU WANT

> *"Now when the queen of Sheba heard of the fame of Solomon concerning the name of the Lord, she came to test him with hard questions... King Solomon gave to the queen of Sheba all she desired, whatever she asked." (1 Kings 10:1, 13)*

When I taught music to my kindergarteners, they had no issue asking questions. There was a waterfall of questions for every class. I had moments of overwhelm, but for the most part, I enjoyed their inquisitive minds and appreciated their desire to know more. The Bible tells us that the Queen of Sheba didn't just show up at Solomon's court with gifts; she came with questions. She wanted to test his wisdom and gauge his leadership skills.

And guess what? She wasn't shy about it! She used her voice, asserted her authority, and demanded answers. The Bible even mentions Solomon fulfilling "every desire she expressed" (1 Kings 10:13).

The Queen of Sheba teaches us a powerful lesson: don't be afraid to use your voice and speak up for what you want. Whether it's a promotion at work, a clear boundary in a relationship, or simply expressing your needs, don't be afraid to be heard. Don't be scared to ask questions. There's a difference between demanding and respectfully asking. Channel your inner Queen of Sheba and use your voice with clarity, confidence, and a touch of regality.

Think of yourself as a queen, ruling over your own life. You can ask for what you deserve, negotiate, and advocate for yourself. Don't be afraid to have difficult conversations and express your desires confidently.

The Gem Being Dropped:

Your voice is a powerful tool, sis. Use it to articulate your needs, set boundaries, and create your desired life. Don't be afraid to ask for what you want, and don't settle for anything less.

6

IT'S OKAY TO DATE OUT OF YOUR COMFORTABLE CIRCLE: SOMETIMES, LOVE DOESN'T SPEAK THE SAME LANGUAGE

"Now when the queen of Sheba heard of the fame of Solomon concerning the name of the Lord, she came to test him with hard questions. She came to Jerusalem with a very great retinue, with camels that bore spices, very much gold, and precious stones. And when she came to Solomon, she spoke with him about all that was in her heart." (1 Kings 10:1-2)

While a bit vague in the details, the Bible suggests that the Queen of Sheba traveled a great distance to meet King Solomon. This wasn't just a casual visit to a neighbor but a journey into unfamiliar territory.

Some might interpret this as strictly political. But let's get real. But let's get real—meeting a powerful ruler from a different culture would undoubtedly bring intrigue, curiosity, and maybe even a spark of connection.

The Queen of Sheba teaches us a powerful lesson: don't be afraid to step outside your comfort zone when it comes to love. Maybe you've always dated people from a similar background. But what about that charming guy with a foreign accent? Or the intriguing man with a completely different perspective on life? Love often grows in the tension between familiarity and the thrill of discovering something—or someone—new.

In nature, cross-pollination serves as a perfect example. When plants are pollinated by pollen from a different species or variety, it often produces stronger, more resilient offspring. Similarly, relationships that bridge cultural or social divides can be rich and rewarding, fostering growth and mutual understanding. This doesn't mean it's always easy; cultural differences can bring unique challenges. But those differences can also deepen your connection, teaching you both to see the world from new angles.

Consider Meghan Markle and Prince Harry. Their love story challenged centuries of rigid royal traditions and cultural expectations. Meghan, an African American actress, brought a fresh, modern perspective to a centuries-old institution. Their union wasn't without its struggles, but it also exemplified the beauty of embracing love across perceived divides. Like the Queen of Sheba, Meghan stepped into unfamiliar territory and helped redefine what was possible in love and partnership.

Think of yourself as a queen exploring the vast world of possibilities. Love can blossom in the most unexpected places, and the courage to step outside your comfortable circle may lead to something extraordinary. Don't limit yourself by rigid ideas of who's "your type." Be open to new experiences and connections that may surprise you.

It's not about abandoning your values or compromising who you are, but rather expanding your view of what love can look like.

The Gem Being Dropped:

Open your heart to love in all its diverse forms. Don't let cultural differences hold you back from a potentially fulfilling relationship. Embrace the adventure, and who knows, you might find your happily ever after in the most unexpected place.

TIME TO DROP YOUR OWN GEMS:

- Reflect on your relationships—are there any standards or values you've compromised? How can you redefine these standards to honor your worth and make healthier choices?

- In what areas of your life do you feel you're over-giving without receiving enough in return? What boundaries can you set to ensure you give from a place of strength, not self-sacrifice?

- Queen Sheba embraced her power and showed up confidently. What aspects of yourself—skills, personality traits, or experiences—are you hiding or minimizing? How can you own your unique power and bring these parts of yourself forward?

- Are there areas where you've hesitated to step outside your comfort zone, especially in relationships or career pursuits? What steps can you take to explore new possibilities?

- Reflect on when you were afraid to speak up for yourself. What held you back, and how can Queen Sheba's story inspire you to use your voice assertively and confidently in the future?

♦ Consider where you invest your time, energy, and resources. Are these investments aligned with your purpose and growth? What changes can you make to ensure you give in ways that uplift yourself and others?

18

LESSONS FROM THE SHULAMMITE WOMAN

Location: The Shulammite woman was from Shulem or Shunem, a town likely located in the northern region of Israel (Song of Solomon 6:13). Shunem was near Mount Gilboa and the Jezreel Valley.

RELATIONSHIP STATUS: MADLY IN LOVE

FAST FACTS:

- The Shulammite woman is the central female figure in Song of Solomon and represents romantic, mutual love.
- She speaks candidly about her attraction, desires, and admiration for her beloved, breaking cultural norms with her open expressions of love.
- Her beauty and devotion are celebrated. She is known for her poetic language and imagery, which paint a picture of deep emotional and physical connection.

- The Song of Solomon is often seen as an allegory of God's love for His people or Christ's love for the Church. In this divine relationship, the Shulammite woman symbolizes the beloved.

LIFE EVENTS:

- She and her beloved engage in a beautiful courtship, expressing longing, affection, and admiration for each other through poetic exchanges (Song of Solomon 1-2).
- At one point, she searches for her beloved in the city, showcasing her devotion and longing to be near him (Song of Solomon 3:1-4).
- She experiences insecurities about her appearance, mentioning her "darkened" skin from working in the vineyards, yet her beloved reassures her of her beauty (Song of Solomon 1:5-6, 2:2).
- Her commitment and desire for balanced, enduring love are evident. She calls for love to be awakened at its right time and celebrated fully (Song of Solomon 2:7, 8:4).

THE WOMEN WHO CAN RELATE:

- Women who want to embrace and celebrate their sensuality and femininity as a divinely created part of who they are.
- Women who long for deep, intimate connections and are waiting patiently for love to come to fruition in its time.

- ◆ Women learning to appreciate and love their bodies, moving past insecurities and societal standards to see themselves as beautifully and wonderfully made.

- ◆ Women who wrestle with balancing the desire to express physical beauty and sensuality while honoring their spiritual identity.

- ◆ Women who value open communication about desires, needs, and boundaries in relationships, building mutual respect and genuine intimacy.

- ◆ Women who've grown up with conflicting messages about sexuality and are exploring a God-honoring, healthy perspective on love and intimacy.

- ◆ Women who have felt pressure to suppress their desires or imaginations due to religious or cultural teachings are finding freedom in seeing them as natural and God-given.

- ◆ Women who believe in the beauty of love being awakened "in its time" and understand that true intimacy grows when nurtured with patience and care.

- ◆ Women who value emotional intimacy and connection, seeking to express themselves openly and authentically in their relationships.

- ◆ Women who see love as sacred and cherish its ability to engage the heart, mind, body, and soul.

I was in sixth grade when I wrote something so vivid, so descriptive, that my teacher called my mother out of concern. We had been assigned to write a play or skit for our creative writing class, and I, fully embracing my young creative genius, decided to write about Mary giving birth to Jesus. But not in the way Christmas pageants present it—with a serene Mary, a clean stable, and a sweetly swaddled baby Jesus. No, I wrote it how I imagined it actually happened: with blood, with screaming, with the full intensity of childbirth in a barn. I went deep into the details—messy, raw, real. My teacher, bless her heart, was alarmed. She worried something was wrong with me, that I had been exposed to something dark or inappropriate. My mother had to reassure her that I was fine—I was just a writer. A writer unafraid to tell the truth.

That sixth-grade moment comes to mind as I introduce you to this chapter. Because once again, I'm going to be descriptive. I'm going to be vivid. And for some, that might be unsettling. But here's what I need you to understand: The Shulammite Woman in Song of Solomon was vivid, too. She did not hold back. She used rich, poetic, sensory language to describe her desires, her beauty, her longing, and her love. She painted pictures with words that made readers feel, taste, and see the passion in her poetry. She was not ashamed of her sensuality. She did not filter her words to make others comfortable. And so, to honor her story, I will not filter mine either.

So, this is your disclaimer: If you have been conditioned to believe that discussing sensuality, intimacy, and the body—especially from a biblical perspective—is taboo, this chapter may challenge you. If you think the Bible only speaks in metaphors about love and not in tangible, physical, and yes, even erotic ways, this chapter may stretch your understanding. But if you are ready to embrace the fullness of God's design, to see the beauty of the human experience through the lens of Scripture, and to reclaim the parts of yourself that you've been told to silence, then welcome. You're exactly where you need to be.

Like my sixth-grade self, I refuse to sanitize the truth. And just like the Shulammite Woman, I refuse to hold back.

1

EMBRACE AND EXPLORE YOUR SENSUALITY

"Behold, you are fair, my love! Behold, you are fair! You have dove's eyes behind your veil. Your hair is like a flock of goats, going down from Mount Gilead. Your teeth are like a flock of shorn sheep..." (Song of Solomon 4:1-3)

There are magnifying glasses all over my mom's house now. Big ones, small ones, and ones with added lighting. It's because they help with being able to see. They amplify what's challenging to observe. The Shulammite Woman invites us to fully embrace the contours of our bodies, the sensations we experience, and the beauty of our physicality—without shame. Her story in scripture allows us to explore our bodies in a way that's not rooted in sinfulness or feeling dirty. The Shulammite is a woman unabashedly in touch with her physical desires. She revels in descriptions of her beauty, comparing her body parts to luscious fruits and powerful animals (Song of Songs 4:1-3). In a time when female beauty is either weaponized or downplayed, The Shulammite Woman throws that notion out the window. She takes ownership of her physicality, celebrating it as a gift from God. And the celebration of her body is not always rooted in her proximity to a man. She embraces and explores her sensuality because she's a female human being. As a woman of God, The Shulammite Woman gives us the green light to make a sensual living a way of life.

In the S5 lifestyle, sensuality is one of the five pillars I teach about, rooted in the understanding that your senses—how you experience the world through touch, taste, sight, smell, and sound—are divine gifts. Sensuality is about being fully present in your body and savoring the beauty, joy, and sacredness of creation. It's not solely about sexuality but about living in tune with the fullness of life, connecting deeply with yourself, others, and God.

Some might argue that focusing on physical beauty diminishes a woman's inner worth. But appreciating our bodies and expressing our sensuality doesn't diminish our other qualities. It's about celebrating the whole package—the physical alongside the spiritual and intellectual.

Key Principles of Sensuality in the S5 Lifestyle:

- ◆ It's About Presence, Not Performance:
  Sensuality is rooted in being present in your body and the world around you, not performing for others or seeking external validation.
- ◆ It's a Gift from God:
  Your ability to experience pleasure, beauty, and connection is

part of God's design. Sensuality celebrates the sacredness of your senses.

♦ It Honors Your Body:

Sensuality teaches you to listen to your body, care for it, and respect its needs and boundaries.

♦ It's Empowering, Not Shameful:

Living sensually helps you move past shame and embrace your body and experiences as part of God's good creation.

♦ It Deepens Your Connection with God:

Sensuality can be an act of worship, where you thank God for the ability to experience the world fully and marvel at the intricacy of His design.

The Gem Being Dropped:

Our bodies are not objects of shame but instruments of pleasure and connection. Let's shed the layers of societal expectations and embrace the sensuality that resides within each of us. When we reclaim our sensuality as sacred and God-honoring, we step into a life of wholeness, joy, and freedom.

2

IT'S OKAY TO LONG FOR LOVE: A DESIRE WORTH CHERISHING

1 By night on my bed, I sought the one I love; I sought him, but I did not find him.

2 "I will rise now," I said, "And go about the city; In the streets and in the squares, I will seek the one I love." I sought him, but I did not find him. 3 The watchmen who go about the city found me; I said, "Have you seen the one I love?" (Song of Solomon 3:1-3)

When your body starts to run low on water, it sends a message to your brain saying, "Hey, we need more water!" That message makes you feel thirsty. It's your body's way of telling you to grab a drink because your body desires to be satisfied. Your body desires to have its thirst quenched. Similar to your body desiring water, it's normal for women to desire emotional and physical intimacy. You're not being weird or unsanctified when you have dreams, thoughts, and urges. You're actually being normal.

The Shulammite's story is a love song, a testament to a yearning for deep connection. She longs for her beloved, venturing out at night to search for him (Song of Songs 3:1-4). What's beautiful about the Song of Songs is that there's more emphasis on longing for love than fulfillment of love. It's like she's constantly hoping, dreaming, longing for the intimacy of her lover. She gives us permission to acknowledge and embrace our desires for intimacy without shame, even if there's no immediate chance of experiencing a fulfillment of that desire in the immediate future. I like how David Carr explains it:

Yet, here, as at so many other points of the Song of Songs, the poetry tantalizes us with the probability of their embrace. She yearns for him to kiss her with his mouth. She exalts his lovemaking over wine. She tells him to take her and run with her, and he brings her into his room. She calls on him to join her in dancing, exclaiming "rightly [those young women! love you." The lovers converse back and forth, go out to the garden, and even lie together in close embrace, but the scene fades with a refrain before anything more happens. The poetry soon shifts to another scene, and we are left teased by these evocations of desire.

(The Erotic Word: Sexuality, Spirituality, and the Bible)

If you find yourself longing for love, intimacy, and connection with someone special, the Shulammite woman sees you and understands all you're feeling.

"YOU'RE NOT BEING WEIRD OR UNSANCTIFIED
WHEN YOU HAVE DREAMS, THOUGHTS, AND URGES.
YOU'RE ACTUALLY BEING NORMAL."

The Gem Being Dropped:

Sisters, there's nothing wrong with longing for love. It's a beautiful human desire, a yearning for connection and companionship. Embrace that longing, nurture it, and don't settle for anything less than a love that sets your soul on fire.

3

EMBRACE THE FULLNESS OF INTIMACY

> *"Like an apple tree among the trees of the woods, so is my beloved among the sons. I sat down in his shade with great delight, and his fruit was sweet to my taste." (Song of Solomon 2:3)*

This might be a point some find surprising, but the Song of Songs offers suggestive imagery that some scholars interpret as alluding to oral sex (Song of Songs 7:1-9). Now, before you get flustered, consider this: While the concept of "sex," as we understand it today, wasn't explicitly discussed, marital intimacy in ancient Israel encompassed a range of physical expressions.

In his book, The Erotic Word: Sexuality, Spirituality, and the Bible, David Carr states, "Judaism celebrates marital love and sex between spouses. Some Jewish laws stipulate that a Jewish Man must be willing to have sex with his wife on Sabbath eve, even if he refrains on other days of the week."

The Song of Songs, with its focus on mutual pleasure, hints at a more expansive view of sexuality than just procreation. Scholars and readers have interpreted some passages to allude to various forms of physical intimacy, including oral sex.

Here are some of the verses that suggest oral physical intimacy.

Song of Solomon 2:3 (NRSV):

> *"As an apple tree among the trees of the wood, so is my beloved among young men. With great delight, I sat in his shadow, and his fruit was sweet to my taste."*

♦ The imagery of tasting the fruit can be seen as a metaphor for oral pleasure.

Song of Solomon 4:16 (NRSV):

> *"Awake, O north wind, and come, O south wind! Blow upon my garden that its fragrance may be wafted abroad. Let my beloved come to his garden and eat its choicest fruits."*

♦ The garden is often interpreted as a metaphor for the woman's body, and the reference to eating its fruits might be understood as a poetic allusion to oral sex.

Song of Solomon 7:7-9 (NRSV):

> *"You are stately as a palm tree, and your breasts are like its clusters. I say I will climb the palm tree and lay hold of its branches. Oh, may your breasts be like clusters of the vine, and the scent of your breath like apples, and your kisses like the best wine that goes down smoothly, gliding over lips and teeth."*

♦ The sensual imagery and, the description of the lover's kisses and the smoothness of wine can be seen as a metaphor for intimate acts.

Some might argue that certain sexual acts are inherently sinful. Paul, however, is clear about Christian liberty. Romans 14:14 (NRSV): "I know and am persuaded in the Lord Jesus that nothing is unclean in itself, but it is unclean for anyone who thinks it unclean." Paul's teaching on Christian liberty emphasizes that what is considered unclean is often a matter of personal conviction. If a couple doesn't view oral sex as unclean or sinful, they may exercise their freedom in Christ to engage in it within the bounds of their marriage.

The focus in relationships should be on mutual respect, love, and commitment within a loving God-honoring relationship. The key is open communication and honoring each other's desires as long as they are consensual.

The Gem Being Dropped:

Sisters, physical intimacy is a beautiful part of a healthy relationship. It's about exploring pleasure together and discovering what brings you and your partner joy. Don't be afraid to communicate your desires and experiment within the boundaries of your comfort and commitment.

SEXUAL IMAGINATION IS NOT ALWAYS SINFUL

Philippians 4:8 (NKJV) "Finally, brethren, whatever things are true, whatever things are noble, whatever things are just, whatever things are pure, whatever things are lovely, whatever things are of good report, if there is any virtue and if there is anything praiseworthy— meditate on these things."

Alright, let's take our time here because this is a hot topic. What's generally accepted in Christian circles is that thinking about sex, unless you're married, is wrong and to be avoided because if you're thinking about it, you're more likely to act on it.

Traditional Christianity teaches that thinking about sexual thoughts leads to deviance, lust, consuming porn, etc. In many instances, our teachings around thinking about sex are rooted in fear and shame rather than liberty and the freedom we have in Christ.

I challenge us to revisit this mindset in light of the Song of Solomon. This book is poetry and allegorical in nature. That means it wasn't reality but the figment of the writer's imagination. The poetry writing also points to the physical intimacy not actually happening but something that was imagined or dreamed. The Song of Songs is filled with vivid metaphors and imagery, showcasing her active imagination (Song of Songs 5:1-8). The Song of Songs, with its evocative language, suggests that a healthy relationship thrives on physical touch, emotional connection, and a healthy dose of sexual fantasy. Further, the ambiguity of the text allows for multiple interpretations regarding marital status. The Shulammite's marital status remains a matter of scholarly debate. Some argue for marriage, others for being betrothed, and others consider them unmarried. With that in mind, it's irresponsible to condemn people who have a vivid erotic imagination regardless of relationship status. Sexual imagination, like any other aspect of our humanity, is part of the complex way God created us. While the Bible does command us to bring our thoughts into captivity to Christ (2 Corinthians 10:5), it also acknowledges the role of our imagination and the importance of understanding it within the broader context of our faith.

Being made in God's image includes the ability to think, imagine, and create. Imagination itself is a neutral faculty that can be used for good or bad. Sexual imagination, when aligned with God's intentions for sexuality, is part of our God-given creativity and humanity. It's not the imagination itself that is sinful, but how it's used. Some might worry that sexual fantasies are a gateway to infidelity. Here's the distinction: fantasies are explorations within the confines of your mind. As long as you communicate openly with your partner and prioritize real-life Intimacy, your imagination, led by the Holy Spirit, can be a powerful tool for strengthening your connection. A popular text used to refute our mind's thinking about sex is Matthew 5:28. "But I tell you that anyone who looks at a woman lustfully has already committed adultery with her in his heart." Jesus' teaching here emphasizes the intent of the heart rather than the mere act of imagining. Sexual thoughts become sinful when they are used to fuel lust or objectification. However, the presence of sexual thoughts or imagination isn't automatically sinful—it's the purpose and focus of those thoughts that matter.

"But Pastor Kim, if I'm not married, are all my sexual thoughts sinful because I'm thinking about someone who is not my spouse?" No. If you're unmarried, it's encouraged to be a steward of your thoughts and manage them well so that your thoughts don't lead to covetousness, envy, jealousy, selfishness, or anything that doesn't represent the heart of God. It's about balancing your natural desires with your spiritual goals, recognizing that your imagination is part of your humanity, and learning to channel it in ways that honor God. Proverbs 4:23 says - "Above all else, guard your heart, for everything you do flows from it." While it's natural to have sexual thoughts, guarding your heart and mind means being mindful of where those thoughts take you. If your sexual imagination is leading to unhealthy fantasies or temptations, it's important to redirect your thoughts toward things that are pure and life-giving (Philippians 4:8).

"SEXUAL IMAGINATION, LIKE ANY OTHER ASPECT OF OUR HUMANITY, IS PART OF THE COMPLEX WAY GOD CREATED US."

The Gem Being Dropped:

A sexual imagination, in itself, is not inherently sinful, as it is part of the natural human experience and creativity with which God created us. Sexual thoughts only become problematic when they lead to objectification, lust, or behaviors that oppose God's values, such as jealousy or selfishness. Whether married or unmarried, steward your thoughts responsibly and align them with God's intentions for sexuality. Ultimately, sexual imagination can be positive and life-giving when directed with the purpose of honoring God, fostering genuine connections, and respecting the dignity of oneself and others.

TIME TO DROP YOUR OWN GEMS:

- How comfortable are you with embracing and exploring your sensuality? Are there any past experiences, teachings, or beliefs that make this challenging? How can you begin to celebrate your body as a sacred gift from God?

- The Shulammite woman longed deeply for connection. Reflect on a time when you longed for love, intimacy, or companionship. How can you embrace and honor that longing as a beautiful, natural part of who you are, even if it hasn't yet been fulfilled?

- What aspects of your body and appearance do you love, and what aspects are harder to appreciate? How can you take small steps towards seeing yourself as beautifully made, both inside and out?

- In what ways do you feel pressured to "downplay" or "hide" your desires, whether emotional, physical, or spiritual? How can you begin to embrace these desires in a healthy way that honors your relationship with God and your sense of self?

♦ How do you currently view the role of imagination in your love life? Do you allow yourself to envision positive, intimate connections? If not, what holds you back, and how can you gently challenge yourself to bring more imagination and openness to your relationships?

♦ Reflect on a time when you have communicated your desires in a relationship— whether physical, emotional, or spiritual. Were you met with understanding and respect? How can you create a safe space for open, honest communication with a future or current partner?

♦ The Shulammite woman's story shows the power of valuing physical beauty and deep connection. How can you balance nurturing your own sense of beauty and sensuality with seeking or building a love that fulfills you emotionally, intellectually, and spiritually?

19

LESSONS FROM QUEEN JEZEBEL

Location: Jezebel was originally from Phoenicia, specifically Sidon, but she moved to Samaria in the northern kingdom of Israel after marrying King Ahab (1 Kings 16:31).

RELATIONSHIP STATUS: MARRIED

FAST FACTS:

♦ Jezebel was the daughter of Ethbaal, king of the Sidonians, and was a high- ranking princess before her marriage to Ahab.

♦ She was deeply devoted to Baal worship and brought her religion to Israel, financially supporting over 800 prophets of Baal and Asherah (1 Kings 18:19).

♦ Jezebel is often associated with manipulation and control, as she used her influence over Ahab to promote her religious practices, challenge Israel's prophets, and secure her power.

♦ Despite her controversial reputation, Jezebel's story reveals a strong-willed woman navigating intense opposition and maintaining her cultural and religious identity in a foreign land.

LIFE EVENTS:

- Marriage to Ahab brought her into Israel, where she influenced Ahab to introduce Baal worship, leading to tension with the prophets of Yahweh and Israel's people (1 Kings 16:31-33).

- Jezebel orchestrated the killing of the prophets of Yahweh and directly opposed Elijah, leading to a famous showdown on Mount Carmel between Elijah and the prophets of Baal (1 Kings 18:4, 19).

- She was involved in the murder of Naboth to secure his vineyard for Ahab, a blatant abuse of power that showed her ruthlessness in achieving her aims (1 Kings 21:5-16).

- Jehu's rebellion eventually led to her downfall, and in her final moments, Jezebel dressed herself and faced Jehu with dignity, even as she knew her death was imminent. She was thrown from a window, fulfilling Elijah's prophecy of her gruesome end (2 Kings 9:30-37).

THE WOMEN WHO CAN RELATE:

- Women who have experienced misjudgment and stereotypes based on their assertiveness, cultural differences, or religious beliefs.

- Women navigating inter-religious relationships or who've experienced cultural tension, feeling pressured to abandon parts of their identity for the sake of acceptance.

♦ Women who've faced unfair labels or societal judgments, particularly around their sexuality or independence, want to reclaim their power and dignity.

♦ Women who recognize the importance of setting boundaries and knowing when to hold others accountable without enabling destructive behavior.

♦ Women who seek to redefine power for themselves—not as dominance or control, but as inner strength, resilience, and integrity in the face of challenge.

♦ Women who have been seen as "too much" or "too bold" but understand the value of standing firm in their beliefs and identities, using wisdom and strength rather than manipulation.

Jezebel. A name that's been tossed around like a flaming torch at a Las Vegas show for centuries. Her name sparks controversy, conjuring images of a wicked temptress or power-hungry queen. But is that all she was? History has painted Jezebel as a villain, but her story is far more complex. A foreign princess from Phoenicia, Jezebel married King Ahab and brought her culture and religion with her—challenging Israel's traditions in ways that made her both a queen and a target.

Jezebel's tale isn't just about manipulation or power plays; it's a mirror reflecting our own struggles as women navigating societal judgment, complex relationships, and the tension between owning our identity and conforming to expectations. Through her story, we can explore the strength, intelligence, and even the mistakes of a queen who dared to live boldly in a man's world. Jezebel's legacy challenges us to rethink power, femininity, and the narratives that define us.

INTER-RELIGIOUS MARRIAGES CAN BE DIFFICULT

> *1 Kings 16:31 (NKJV): "And it came to pass, as though it had been a trivial thing for him to walk in the sins of Jeroboam the son of Nebat, that he took as wife Jezebel the daughter of Ethbaal, king of the Sidonians; and he went and served Baal and worshiped him."*

Jezebel was a queen in a tough spot, trying to navigate a foreign land with her own beliefs. Let me put this in perspective: Jezebel was a princess. Her father gave her away in marriage to a man she didn't know, and she was forced to leave the place of her birth and the religion of her childhood. She was devoted to her god, so much so that she financially supported over 800 prophets of her religion.

Jezebel was brought to Israel to marry. She had no option. Raised to honor the deities of her native land of Canaan, her chief deity was Baal. The writer blames Jezebel for Ahab's idolatry, but I want to emphasize that Jezebel was simply faithful to the religion of her childhood. She refused to surrender her identity or submerge herself in the religion of her husband's people. They had an inter-religious marriage. It was a political alliance.

Inter-religious marriages can indeed be challenging, as they often involve more than just the union of two individuals—they bring together different belief systems, cultural backgrounds, and sometimes conflicting values. Jezebel's story provides a vivid example of how these dynamics can play out in a relationship.

When two people come from different religious backgrounds, they may have fundamentally different beliefs about life, purpose, morality, and the afterlife. These differences can create tension, especially regarding major life decisions like raising children, observing religious holidays, or participating in religious communities. For instance, one partner might believe in regular worship attendance, while the other might not see it as necessary, leading to disagreements.

Religion is often intertwined with cultural identity. When individuals marry across religious lines, they may also be marrying into a different cultural context, which can lead to feelings of isolation or the loss of one's cultural identity. Jezebel, for example, struggled with maintaining her cultural and religious identity in a foreign land where her practices were not only unfamiliar but actively opposed. This mirrors the modern challenge of balancing the preservation of one's cultural and religious heritage while embracing a new, often conflicting, set of traditions.

Family and community expectations can put immense pressure on inter-religious marriages. Both partners might face opposition from their families, who may have strong opinions about marrying within the faith. This can lead to feelings of alienation or guilt, particularly if the marriage is seen as a betrayal of one's upbringing or religious commitments. Jezebel's marriage was politically motivated, but in many cases today, family pressure can play a similar role, pushing individuals into or away from certain relationships based on religious expectations.

For many people, spiritual connection is a crucial component of marital intimacy. When spouses do not share the same faith, achieving the deep spiritual bond that many couples desire can be difficult. This lack of spiritual unity can sometimes lead to a sense of emotional distance, as one partner might feel that a significant part of their life and identity is not fully shared or understood by the other. Jezebel and Ahab's marriage was marked by spiritual disunity, with each adhering to their own gods, ultimately contributing to their union's downfall.

Inter-religious marriages require a great deal of mutual respect, open communication, and compromise. They can be successful but often involve navigating complex issues related to belief systems, cultural identities, family expectations, and societal pressures. Just as Jezebel and Ahab's marriage was fraught with challenges due to their differing religious commitments, modern inter-religious couples must also work hard to find common ground and build a life together that honors both of their backgrounds.

The Gem Being Dropped:

Use wisdom when marrying someone whose religion is not the same as yours.

2

REJECT THE JEZEBEL SEXUAL STEREOTYPE

So God created mankind in his own image, in the image of God he created them; male and female he created them. (Genesis 1:27 NIV)

Exploring different aspects of Jezebel's story isn't about changing the narrative but rather about understanding the full depth and complexity of biblical characters. Jezebel is often reduced to a symbol of sexual immorality, but the Bible speaks more about her political power moves than anything related to her sexuality (1 Kings 18:4, 19:1-2). Phyllis Trible, in Texts of Terror, highlights that Jezebel's narrative reflects her political influence and defiance, not primarily her sexuality. She argues that misreading her story contributes to the cultural reduction of powerful women to immoral archetypes.

The myth of Jezebel as a seductress stems from a misinterpretation of 2 Kings 9:22, where the reference to "whoredoms" is not about literal prostitution but rather describes people who are unfaithful to God. Renita J. Weems, in Just a Sister Away, explains that terms like "whoredoms" often signify spiritual unfaithfulness or idolatry rather than literal sexual misconduct. This interpretation challenges traditional, narrow readings that emphasize sexuality over other aspects of Jezebel's story.

This portrayal also reflects a larger societal issue: the tendency to reduce powerful women to their sexuality. The stereotype of Jezebel as a seductress has been historically weaponized, particularly in white culture, to justify the exploitation of Black female bodies. Tricia Rose, in Longing to Tell, underscores how the Jezebel stereotype was historically used to portray Black women as hypersexual and unworthy of respect or protection, allowing white people to exploit them without consequence. Melissa Harris-Perry, in Sister Citizen, further connects this stereotype to the broader societal tendency to police and shame Black women's bodies and sexuality, showing how these harmful narratives persist and influence perceptions of Black women's worth and autonomy.

Understanding this helps us avoid oversimplifying complex biblical figures like Jezebel. The seductress label not only distorts her story but also impacts our own sense of sexual power and freedom. Jacquelyn Grant, in White Women's Christ and Black Women's Jesus, calls for a reclamation of sexuality as sacred and God-given, challenging the harmful stereotypes that distort women's identities and autonomy. By rejecting the Jezebel stereotype, we can begin to dismantle the harmful associations imposed on women for centuries and, instead, celebrate the full range of our identities—including our sexual selves—without shame or fear.

"YOU'RE FREE TO REJECT NEGATIVE JEZEBEL STEREOTYPES AROUND YOUR SEXUALITY."

The Gem Being Dropped:

You're free to reject negative Jezebel stereotypes around your sexuality. God created our sexuality as something beautiful and powerful (Song of Solomon 4:7). He wants us to embrace our sensuality without shame, rejecting the notion that a woman's worth is tied to her sexuality.

3

IT'S OKAY TO WEAR MAKEUP

"Now when Jehu had come to Jezreel, Jezebel heard of it; and she put paint on her eyes and adorned her head, and looked through a window." (2 Kings 9:30)

For too long, Jezebel's decision to put on makeup before her death has been preached as a symbol of vanity and wickedness. This interpretation has led countless women to shy away from makeup, jewelry, or any form of outward adornment, fearing that it might be seen as sinful or superficial. But let's pause for a moment and reconsider this narrative. When Jezebel "painted her eyes and adorned her head" (2 Kings 9:30), it wasn't just an act of vanity. This wasn't about seduction, nor was it a desperate attempt to charm her way out of a grim fate. No, Jezebel was a queen who understood that her end was near and chose to face it with dignity and courage on her own terms.

In her final moments, Jezebel wasn't trying to impress Jehu; she was standing tall, even as she knew the tide had turned against her. She threw the Zimri insult, a sharp reminder of the fleeting power of those who betray—Zimri being the man who ruled for only seven days before his own downfall. Jezebel wasn't begging for mercy; she was asserting her identity as a queen, even as the world around her collapsed. She was like many female politicians or activists today who, under intense public scrutiny and personal attacks, maintain their composure and dignity. They are often criticized for their appearance or for daring to maintain their personal image under pressure, but this criticism misses the point entirely.

Society has long misinterpreted women's self-expression—like wearing makeup—as a sign of vanity, something shallow or frivolous. But it's okay to reclaim these aspects of our lives as expressions of our identity and strength. Makeup isn't just about looking good; it's about feeling good, about facing the world with confidence and grace, even when that world tries to tear you down.

The Gem Being Dropped:

God wants us to appreciate our external expressions as reflections of our inner strength and dignity. We are challenging the social and religious notions that too often misinterpret a woman's self-care as vanity. Sisters, it's time to take back the narrative. Your beauty and adornment is not a sign of weakness or vanity—it's a declaration of your God-given strength, dignity, and identity. So wear that makeup, and do it unapologetically, knowing that you are honoring the woman God created you to be.

4

BEWARE OF ENABLING DESTRUCTIVE BEHAVIORS

"But there was no one like Ahab who sold himself to do wickedness in the sight of the Lord, because Jezebel his wife stirred him up." (1 Kings 21:25)

Jezebel's unwavering support of her husband, Ahab, ultimately fueled his downfall. Instead of guiding him toward righteousness, she enabled his destructive behaviors. One striking example is when Ahab coveted Naboth's vineyard. Jezebel manipulated the situation by orchestrating Naboth's murder to satisfy Ahab's desires, showing how enabling someone's harmful choices can lead to devastating consequences.

This isn't just ancient history. Studies show that enabling behavior often stems from a desire to avoid conflict or maintain harmony in relationships. For example, a 2021 study on relational dynamics found that individuals who enabled harmful behaviors—like substance abuse or unethical actions—often did so out of fear of rejection or a perceived obligation to "support" their loved ones. However, this misplaced support often perpetuates cycles of harm.

As women, we are natural encouragers, often seeking to uplift those we care about. But Jezebel's story is a cautionary tale: support doesn't mean silence. Real love requires the courage to speak the truth, even when it's uncomfortable. When we enable destructive behaviors, we risk harming the other person and compromising our integrity and spiritual growth.

Imagine a friend drowning in debt because of reckless spending. Encouraging her to get another loan instead of addressing the root problem might feel supportive at the moment but ultimately reinforces harmful patterns. True support would involve guiding her toward better financial habits, even if it means having a difficult conversation.

"SUPPORTING SOMEONE DOESN'T MEAN ENABLING HARMFUL CHOICES!"

The Gem Being Dropped:

Supporting someone doesn't mean enabling harmful choices. Real love sometimes means speaking the truth, even when it's uncomfortable.

REDEFINE WHAT POWER
MEANS FOR YOU

"So it happened, when Joram saw Jehu, that he said, 'Is it peace, Jehu?' So he answered, 'What peace, as long as the harlotries of your mother Jezebel and her witchcraft are so many?'" (2 Kings 9:22)

"Yet it shall not be so among you; but whoever desires to become great among you, let him be your servant. And whoever desires to be first among you, let him be your slave." (Matthew 20:26-27)

Jezebel's story exemplifies power rooted in control, manipulation, and domination. Her pursuit of power wasn't about serving others but maintaining dominance at all costs, leading to her ultimate downfall. Her life challenges us to reconsider how we define and use power in our own lives.

In today's world, power is often seen through the lens of influence, wealth, or status. According to the study 'Empathetic Leadership: How Leader Emotional Support and Understanding

Impact Management and Job Performance' (2019), leaders who prioritize service, empathy, and collaboration inspire loyalty and achieve long-term success more effectively than those who rely on control or fear. This aligns with Jesus' teaching that true greatness comes through servanthood, not domination.

Imagine a leader who uses her position to elevate her team, nurturing their growth and success. Compare that to a leader who micromanages and intimidates to maintain control. The former creates an environment of trust and collaboration, while the latter breeds resentment and dysfunction.

For women, Jezebel's story reminds us to reject the worldly view of power rooted in selfishness. Instead, we are called to embrace power that reflects God's character—power rooted in love, humility, and purpose. True power isn't about controlling others but empowering them. It's the quiet strength to persevere, the courage to lead with compassion, and the resilience to live in alignment with godly values.

The Gem Being Dropped:

Real power is about the strength of character, not control. Embrace a power that lifts others up, honors God, and strengthens your spirit.

TIME TO DROP YOUR OWN GEMS:

♦ Jezebel maintained her cultural and religious identity despite intense pressure. Are there parts of your identity or beliefs that you've felt pressured to change for acceptance in relationships or communities? How can you honor these aspects of yourself more fully?

♦ Reflecting on Jezebel's story, where do you feel the societal "Jezebel stereotype" has impacted how you view your sexuality or confidence? How can you start reclaiming a positive and empowered sense of your sensuality?

♦ Have you ever been judged or labeled negatively for being assertive, bold, or confident? How has this affected your sense of self, and what steps can you take to own these qualities unapologetically?

♦ Jezebel's use of makeup before facing her death has been seen as a symbol of dignity and identity. In what ways do you express your identity through your appearance? How might you use self-expression as a source of confidence and inner strength?

- ♦ Reflect on a time you supported someone's choices, even if they went against your values. What did you learn from that experience about healthy support and boundaries?

- ♦ Jezebel's story challenges us to rethink what true power looks like. How do you currently define power in your life? How can you redefine power to be more about inner strength, integrity, and uplifting others?

- ♦ In inter-religious relationships like Jezebel's, profound differences can create tension. How did you navigate those dynamics if you've experienced a relationship with differing values or beliefs? What did you learn about preserving your identity within the relationship?

20

LESSONS FROM THE WOMAN AT THE WELL

Location: The story takes place in Sychar, a town in Samaria near Jacob's well. (John 4:5)

RELATIONSHIP STATUS: COMPLICATED

FAST FACTS:

♦ She was the first person to whom Jesus openly revealed Himself as the Messiah (John 4:26).

♦ Her encounter with Jesus led her to become an evangelist, as she ran back to her town and told everyone about Jesus, leading many to believe in Him (John 4:28-30, 39).

♦ The fact that she came to the well at noon, the hottest part of the day, indicates she was likely trying to avoid others due to her social status or reputation (John 4:6-7).

LIFE EVENTS:

- Encountered Jesus while fetching water from Jacob's well, where He offered her "living water" and spoke about her life in a way that astonished her (John 4:7-14).

- Her conversation with Jesus led her to understand true worship and spiritual transformation, as Jesus told her that the time had come for people to worship God "in spirit and truth" (John 4:23-24).

- Her testimony to the people in her town led to many Samaritans believing in Jesus, showing her immediate impact after her life-changing encounter with Him (John 4:39-42).

THE WOMEN WHO CAN RELATE:

- Women who've been judged for their past or feel like outcasts in society.
- Women who have been married more than once.
- Women who have been in several relationships.
- Women who have trust issues and avoid getting too close because they've been hurt too many times.
- Women who don't mind having men around and can engage with them quite well.
- Women who know their worth and can hold their own in theological conversations.

- ◆ Independent women.

- ◆ Women who have struggled in relationships and experienced heartbreak or brokenness.

- ◆ Women who've had life-changing encounters with God that transformed their sense of self-worth and purpose.

- ◆ Women who desire to be seen for who they truly are, not just for their past mistakes.

- ◆ Women who've found redemption and felt compelled to share their testimony with others.

The woman at the well has been judged for centuries. Some paint her as a scarlet woman, drawing water at noon to avoid the disapproving stares from the village gossip. Others turn her into a caricature of female empowerment, conveniently ignoring the social stigma she likely faced. But we can't fall for these extremes. Let's meet her in the complexity of her story. This encounter at the well overflows with lessons about faith, sex, and relationships. It's a story about a woman on a quest for something more profound, a woman whom Jesus meets not with judgment, but with an invitation to a love that satisfies in a way nothing else can.

ONLY JESUS CAN SATISFY YOUR DESIRES

> *"Jesus answered and said to her, 'Whoever drinks of this water will thirst again, but whoever drinks of the water that I shall give him will never thirst. But the water that I shall give him will become in him a fountain of water springing up into everlasting life.'" (John 4:13-14)*

> *"O God, You are my God; Early will I seek You; My soul thirsts for You; My flesh longs for You in a dry and thirsty land where there is no water." (Psalm 63:1)*

> *"The LORD will guide you continually, and satisfy your soul in drought, and strengthen your bones; you shall be like a watered garden, and like a spring of water, whose waters do not fail." (Isaiah 58:11):*

One of the things I talk about in my ministry, The House of Women, is how to manage your sexual desires when you're single—

and even how to manage them when you're married because not all partners are always down for sexual intimacy. I teach about permitting Jesus to satisfy our desires—not in a physical sense, but in a spiritual one. And notice, I said satisfy, not nullify. We're not asking Jesus to take away our desires; instead, it's been a beautiful experience to invite Yeshua into my sexual decisions, desires, and development. We invite Jesus into everything else, so why not our body's natural desire for sex?

I believe the woman at the well reminds us that Jesus is the one who satisfies. When Jesus enters the scene, He's a radical rabbi, challenging societal norms. He initiates a conversation with our sister, which is a revolutionary act in itself. He offers her "living water," a metaphor for a lasting spiritual connection with God that transcends worldly desires. Jesus is showing this woman—and teaching us—that the true fulfillment of all our needs must first be rooted in our relationship with the Lord. We have to allow ourselves to experience the loving satisfaction of our Lord and what He brings more than external validation or physical intimacy.

I can testify that Jesus doesn't take away our desires but provides safety for them. He helps us manage our desires in healthy ways while acknowledging their sacredness. Christ doesn't condemn, ridicule, or minimize but has compassion—so much compassion that His presence satisfies. This isn't something that can be explained; it must be experienced. This encounter reminds us that true fulfillment comes from a relationship with the divine, not external validation or fleeting physical intimacy.

Think about it. We chase all sorts of things to fill the void in our hearts—relationships, achievements, and that perfect Instagram life. But these things leave us thirsty for more. The woman at the well knew this feeling all too well. Remember, she kept coming back to the well, day after day. That physical thirst mirrored a more profound longing in her soul.

Thankfully, Jesus offers living water that satisfies on a deeper level. It's a love that fills emptiness and has a purpose that transcends fleeting desires. It doesn't mean ignoring your needs, sis. It means finding a love that empowers you to pursue those desires in a healthy, fulfilling way.

The Gem Being Dropped:

Your desires aren't wrong—they're a sign that you were made for more. Don't settle for temporary fixes or fleeting pleasures. Let Jesus show you what it means to be fully satisfied—a satisfaction so deep it transforms how you see yourself, your relationships, and your worth.

"YOUR DESIRES AREN'T WRONG THEY'RE A SIGN THAT YOU WERE MADE FOR MORE."

2

YOUR WORTH DOESN'T COME FROM HOW MANY PARTNERS YOU'VE HAD

"Jesus said to her, 'Go, call your husband, and come here.' The woman answered and said, 'I have no husband.' Jesus said to her, 'You have well said, "I have no husband," for you have had five husbands, and the one whom you now have is not your husband; in that you spoke truly.'" (John 4:16-18)

"But now, thus says the LORD, who created you, O Jacob, and He who formed you, O Israel: 'Fear not, for I have redeemed you; I have called you by your name; You are Mine.'" (Isaiah 43:1)

Shout out to all the girls who have a body count. I see you. More importantly, the woman at the well sees you. And even more importantly, Jesus sees you, and Jesus never condemns the woman's past, and He doesn't condemn you either.

So many of us sat through horrifying sermons and youth meetings that reinforced the idea that our worth and value were diminished because our "rose petals" were used up, or we were like a piece of chewing gum that several people chewed. It's pretty gross stuff.

But I love how Jesus interacts with this woman. First of all, He talks to her openly and publicly. He doesn't make His interaction with her a secret or something to be ashamed of. He speaks to her. He sees her. Acknowledges her. Converses with her. The sun is scorching, while the rules are being broken, but that doesn't stop Jesus from acknowledging her presence simply because she's worthy of living water. She's deserving of God's spirit within her. She's worthy of an encounter with the Divine.

And there's nothing in her past that would stop Jesus from stopping to be with her. She could've slept with one person or 100. She's still worthy of love, acceptance, and adoration. She's still worthy of God's encounters. Why? Because Jesus doesn't define her worth by the number of relationships she's had. This is a powerful message for us, too, sisters. Our value doesn't diminish with every heartbreak or past choice. God sees our hearts, not our history.

Yes, Jesus exposes her past relationships, mentioning her five husbands and the man she's currently with. But graciously, He doesn't condemn her. Instead, He offers her a chance to rewrite her story.

This encounter shatters the lie that our worth is defined by our past choices, especially when it comes to our sexual history. The woman at the well might have felt ostracized by her community, but Jesus sees her with compassion.

The Gem Being Dropped:

Never diminish your value because of your past. You're worthy of love simply by existing. Period.

3

JESUS INCLUDED YOUR SEXUAL PAST WHEN HE CHOSE YOU

"The woman then left her waterpot, went her way into the city, and said to the men, 'Come, see a Man who told me all things that I ever did. Could this be the Christ?' Then they went out of the city and came to Him." (John 4:28-30)

"There is therefore now no condemnation to those who are in Christ Jesus, who do not walk according to the flesh, but according to the Spirit." (Romans 8:1)

> *"But God has chosen the foolish things of the world to put to shame the wise, and God has chosen the weak things of the world to put to shame the things which are mighty; and the base things of the world and the things which are despised God has chosen, and the things which are not, to bring to nothing the things that are, that no flesh should glory in His presence." (1 Corinthians 1:27-29)*

I love that Jesus included a woman with a complex sexual history in a profound theological conversation. That, my sisters, is a radical act of love. And it's a radical act of liberation.

Nowhere in the text does Jesus insist that she repent and ask forgiveness or pray and fast for 30 days before she can testify. She doesn't have to pray special prayers to remove the "soul ties" to the five men and the current man she's with. She doesn't have to be perfect and holy before telling people to come see a man who told me everything about me.

It's because Jesus didn't view her sexual past through the lens of shame. He saw her past through the lens of a testimony—a powerful testimony of overcoming and not allowing her past to define her. Her story qualified her to be an evangelist. Her story qualified her to express her love and excitement about this man who changed her life.

And so, to the woman who God has called to do great work, to change the world, to change your neighborhood, to use your influence to shift cultures, cities, and communities—don't let anyone ever tell you that your past destroys your ability to be used by God to change the world. Don't let anyone gatekeep your ability to share the goodness of God with your neighbors, friends, and loved ones. You have a story—a story of God's love changing you. And God still wants your past to be part of the story because it's a reminder that our humanity is always factored in when God decides who He will use for His glory. The woman at the well might have been navigating her sexuality in a way society disapproved of, but Jesus sees her humanity and her capacity for love.

The Gem Being Dropped:

Never allow your past to restrict or confine how, when, and where God wants to use you. You're not a relic confined to a museum to be observed. You're a living, breathing being with a story that will shift the trajectory of so many lives. Walk into it.

"JESUS DIDN'T VIEW HER SEXUAL PAST THROUGH THE LENS OF SHAME HE SAW IT THROUGH THE LENS OF A TESTIMONY."

MARRIAGE ISN'T REQUIRED FOR SERVICE TO GOD

"And many of the Samaritans of that city believed in Him because of the word of the woman who testified, 'He told me all that I ever did.' So when the Samaritans had come to Him, they urged Him to stay with them; and He stayed there two days. And many more believed because of His own word. Then they said to the woman, 'Now we believe, not because of what you said, for we ourselves have heard Him and we know that this is indeed the Christ, the Savior of the world.'" (John 4:39-42)

"Before I formed you in the womb I knew you; before you were born I sanctified you; I ordained you a prophet to the nations." (Jeremiah 1:5)

You see it on social media—women who are married flaunting their man and giving 'look at me' vibes. Don't get me wrong—be excited, be happy, enjoy the moment. Also, check your heart for any "I'm better than you" residue coming through. And if there is, it's not all your fault. There's so much evidence that marriage is considered a status symbol. It shifts society's perception of your identity. It means you're a good girl who is worthy of being chosen. It suggests that you're better off financially. It means you're worthy of being protected and provided for. Marriage is a come-up in our society.

Some women wear rings in public spaces as a single parent so that they will be treated more equitably and fairly, avoiding judgment for being a single mom. So when Jesus steps onto the scene and addresses this woman living with a man who's not even her husband, it completely flips the script on who's qualified to share the good news of Jesus with the world.

What the woman Jesus spoke to at the well does for us today is shattering the assumption that marriage is a prerequisite for a fulfilling life and service to God. People told me I couldn't have a ministry for women that dealt with being sexy and saved because I wasn't married. I wasn't qualified because I didn't have a man. Well, the woman at the well wasn't married either. Yet Jesus entrusted her with a vital message that shifted her community. The text says she became an evangelist, sharing her encounter with Jesus with the entire Samaritan town.

This story dismantles the idea that a woman's value is tied to her marital status. The woman at the well-found purpose and fulfillment outside the confines of marriage. Her story reminds us that God uses us exactly where we are, regardless of our relationship status.

The Gem Being Dropped:

Your calling doesn't depend on your marital status. You are fearfully and wonderfully made, equipped to serve God and make a difference in the world right now.

TIME TO DROP YOUR OWN GEMS:

- How have you sought fulfillment in the past, and how has Jesus filled a deeper need?
- How has societal pressure or religious messages impacted your view of your desires?
- Do you struggle with shame related to your sexual history? How can this story help you find freedom?
- Have you ever felt judged for your past relationships? How can you embrace God's forgiveness and move forward?
- Do you feel comfortable healthily expressing your sensuality? How can you connect with God through your body?
- Do you feel pressure to get married? How can you find purpose and fulfillment in your life right now?
- How does the story of the woman at the well inspire you to live a more courageous and authentic life?
- What gifts and talents do you have to offer God's kingdom, regardless of your relationship status?

21

LESSONS FROM THE WOMAN CAUGHT IN ADULTERY

Location: In Jerusalem, the capital city of Isra-el, the very heart of religious life in the temple courts (John 8:2)

RELATIONSHIP STATUS: SINGLE & EXPOSED

FAST FACTS:

◆ She was used as a trap set by religious leaders to challenge the authority of Jesus (John 8:3-6)

◆ Her story is one of the best examples of Jesus' mercy, grace, and refusal to condemn people despite the judgment (John 8:7-11)

LIFE EVENTS:

- Caught in the act of adultery by leaders and dragged publicly before Jesus for judgment (John 8:3-4)
- Faced death by stoning according to the law for adultery (John 8:5)
- Jesus wrote in the sand before inviting those who were condemning her to cast the first stone if they've never done wrong (John 8:6-7)
- Jesus told her I don't condemn her either and gave her another chance at life (John 8:10-11)

THE WOMEN WHO CAN RELATE

- Women who have been set up
- Women who have had affairs
- Women who have been exploited
- Women who have been publicly shamed, condemned, or ridiculed for their sexual choices
- Women who long for compassion and understanding from religious and societal institutions but have received judgment instead
- Women caught in toxic or destructive relationships who are in need of healing and restoration.
- Women who feel trapped by their past but are searching for

freedom and a new beginning.

♦ Women who the grace and mercy of God have forever changed

This story, often referred to as the Pericope Adulterae, involves a woman caught in adultery and brought before Jesus by the religious leaders of the time. Have you ever felt the sting of judgmental eyes burning into you? Maybe a past relationship went south, leaving whispers and sideways glances in its wake. Or perhaps you're navigating the complexities of desire and intimacy, yearning for a love that affirms your whole self, sexuality and all. Well, the unnamed woman caught in adultery from the Gospel of John (John 8:3-11) is a kindred spirit. This unnamed sister often gets relegated to a cautionary tale, a stark reminder of the consequences of sin. But what if there's more to her story? What if, through her experience, we can glean gems of wisdom about shame, forgiveness, and embracing our sacred sexuality?

1

YOUR SEXUAL MISTAKES DON'T DEFINE YOU

> *"When Jesus had raised Himself up and saw no one but the woman, He said to her, 'Woman, where are those accusers of yours? Has no one condemned you?' She said, 'No one, Lord.' And Jesus said to her, 'Neither do I condemn you; go and sin no more.'" (John 8:10-11)*

> *"There is therefore now no condemnation to those who are in Christ Jesus, who do not walk according to the flesh, but according to the Spirit." (Romans 8:1)*

United Airlines made a huge mistake that day. Thousands of flights were canceled due to FAA issues, and they lost so much money. It was all over the news. People were tweeting their anger and frustration. It was horrible. Now, before I continue with this story, you must know that I'm fiercely loyal to United. So, I reached out to them because I was one of the people who had my flight canceled repeatedly during this airline fiasco. But I like what United did. They gave me a few thousand air miles, flight credit, and what sounded like a sincere apology. I see that United has bounced back from that flight meltdown, and people are still flying their airline. They didn't allow that mishap to define them. Instead, they used it as an opportunity to clarify who they were.

The first and perhaps most liberating lesson from this passage is the reminder that our mistakes, sexual or otherwise, do not define our worth or identity. Just because people know about your past proclivities doesn't mean you are forever tied to that identity. Jesus' response to the woman's accusers, inviting anyone without sin to cast the first stone, shifts the focus from her actions to the shared human condition of imperfection. This moment underscores the transformative power of grace and the possibility of a fresh start, free from the weight of past mistakes. Imagine the horror of being dragged before the crowd, your transgression plastered across the town square. Shame must have been like a suffocating plastic bag on her shoulders. But sisters, here's what's so beautiful: Jesus doesn't condemn her. In fact, he challenges the very foundation of shame-based judgment. When the crowd, fueled by self-righteousness, wants to stone her, Jesus says something revolutionary: "Let the one who has never sinned throw the first stone" (John 8:7). This powerful statement flips the script. It exposes the hypocrisy of those judging her, reminding them that we all fall short. Our mistakes, sexual or otherwise, don't erase our worth. We deserve love, forgiveness, and a chance to start anew.

The Gem Being Dropped:

Sister, you are not your past mistakes. You are a work of art in progress, worthy of love and grace, no matter your choices.

Remember, God's love is boundless, and it extends even to your messy pieces.

2

BE WARY OF RELIGIOUS MEN USING SEX TO TRAP OR EXPLOIT YOU

"Then the scribes and Pharisees brought to Him a woman caught in adultery. And when they had set her in the midst, they said to Him, 'Teacher, this woman was caught in adultery, in the very act. Now Moses, in the law, commanded us that such should be stoned. But what do You say?' They said, testing Him, that they might have something to accuse Him of. But Jesus stooped down and wrote on the ground with His finger, as though He did not hear." (John 8:3-6)

"'Beware of false prophets, who come to you in sheep's clothing, but inwardly they are ravenous wolves. You will know them by their fruits. Do men gather grapes from thornbushes or figs from thistles?'" (Matthew 7:15-16)

> *"'Woe to you, scribes and Pharisees, hypocrites! For you are like whitewashed tombs which indeed appear beautiful outwardly, but inside are full of dead men's bones and all uncleanness. Even so, you also outwardly appear righteous to men, but inside you are full of hypocrisy and lawlessness.'" (Matthew 23:27-28)*

Oh, the stories I could tell. Men of the cloth, men who profess to be followers and proclaimers of the gospel, are often guilty of using sex to trap sincere women. The rise of awareness of spiritual abuse is necessary because there are countless stories of women who have been used for selfish gain.

One study revealed that 12% of female churchgoers have experienced sexual misconduct or harassment from a church leader (Baylor Religion Survey, 2019). According to a 2018 study by the Faith Trust Institute, over 75% of women abused by clergy report that it severely impacted their trust in God and caused emotional, spiritual, and relational trauma. These men come in the name of godliness as spiritual guides or counselors, only to exploit vulnerability under the guise of compassion, often using the authority they claim from scripture to ultimately comfort you in their bedrooms or church offices.

The actions of the Pharisees in this story serve as a cautionary tale about the dangers of those who wield religion as a tool for manipulation, particularly in matters of sexual activity. These were the very men who were supposed to uphold God's law, yet they used religion as a weapon—a way to shame and control. Their motive wasn't justice; it was to test Jesus, hoping to trap Him in a contradiction. However, the attempt to use the woman's situation as a trap for Jesus reveals deeper hypocrisy and a willingness to exploit individual vulnerabilities for personal or ideological gain.

This lesson calls for discernment and vigilance in recognizing and resisting such exploitation. It also calls for men to hold their brothers in Christ accountable for the foolishness they see but ignore or silently agree with. Studies show that fewer than half of pastors have policies in place to address clergy misconduct, highlighting the lack of accountability that allows exploitation to persist unchecked (Barna Group, 2017). We can no longer tolerate men making church spaces unsafe for women who simply want to exist and not be taken advantage of.

This tactic of using religion to manipulate women's sexuality is as old as time itself. It can take many forms: guilt trips about "impure thoughts," pressure to conform to unrealistic purity standards, or even using scripture to justify controlling behavior in relationships. I've heard men say, "The spirit is willing, but the flesh is weak," to excuse their abusive, manipulative behavior. And yes, I know women can also be complicit in this, but this book aims to address how religious men unfairly and poorly treat women. It needs to stop.

"DON'T LET ANYONE USE RELIGION AS A TOOL TO CONTROL YOUR DESIRES OR MAKE YOU FEEL ASHAMED OF YOUR BODY."

The Gem Being Dropped:

Be discerning, Queen! Don't let anyone use religion as a tool to control your desires or make you feel ashamed of your body. A healthy relationship with God empowers you, celebrates your wholeness, and encourages you to make choices that honor yourself.

3

CHRIST RESTORES OUR SEXUALITY, HE DOESN'T CONDEMN IT

> *"When Jesus had raised Himself up and saw no one but the woman, He said to her, 'Woman, where are those accusers of yours? Has no one condemned you?' She said, 'No one, Lord.' And Jesus said to her, 'Neither do I condemn you; go and sin no more.'" (John 8:10-11)*

> *"Instead of your shame, you shall have double honor, and instead of confusion, they shall rejoice in their portion. Therefore, in their land, they shall possess double; everlasting joy shall be theirs." (Isaiah 61:7)*

I had a favorite pair of high-heeled boots a few years ago that were ruined by the wintry weather. But instead of throwing them away and considering them useless, I took them to a shoemaker who was able to restore my boots to their rightful beauty and shine. Just as the shoemaker restored my boots, in His interaction with the woman, Jesus models a response to sexual decisions rooted in compassion rather than condemnation. By refusing to shame her and instead offering her a path forward—"Go and sin no more"—Jesus affirms the value of sexual integrity while also recognizing the potential for redemption and restoration.

Unlike purity culture, which shames and makes you feel bad for having sexual encounters, Jesus does none of that. He doesn't discard, minimize, or drag this woman. Instead, He covers and restores her publicly. He shames and dismantles the system that shamed and manipulated her in the first place.

Today, there are still systems, institutions, and denominations that refuse to destroy the oppressive, repressive beliefs and mindsets that hold the sexuality of women hostage. But when we look to Jesus, we see a liberator and defender. We see a man of God who extends grace and mercy. It's a radical act of liberation and grace. This encounter illustrates that our sexuality, when embraced within divine love and grace, can be a source of healing and wholeness.

> ### "JESUS DIDN'T VIEW HER SEXUAL PAST THROUGH THE LENS OF SHAME HE SAW IT THROUGH THE LENS OF RESTORATION."

The Gem Being Dropped:

Sister, your sexuality is a sacred part of who you are. It's not something to be hidden or feared. When rooted in love and respect, sexual intimacy can be a beautiful expression of your relationship with your partner.

JESUS HATES SEXUAL INJUSTICE AND MANIPULATION

"So when they continued asking Him, He raised Himself up and said to them, 'He who is without sin among you, let him throw a stone at her first.' And again, He stooped down and wrote on the ground. Then those who heard it, being convicted by their conscience, went out one by one, beginning with the oldest even to the last. And Jesus was left alone, and the woman standing in the midst." (John 8:7-9)

"Learn to do good; seek justice, rebuke the oppressor; defend the fatherless, plead for the widow." (Isaiah 1:17)

"Open your mouth for the speechless, in the cause of all who are appointed to die. Open your mouth, judge righteously, and plead the cause of the poor and needy." (Proverbs 31:8-9)

In God's economy, there's no room for injustice or power imbalances. In our world today, women are losing their rights to reproductive health and bodily autonomy in devastating ways. According to the World Health Organization, an estimated 1 in 3 women will experience physical or sexual violence in their lifetime. The Rape, Abuse & Incest National Network (RAINN) reports that every 9 minutes, someone in the U.S. is sexually assaulted. Many women, both churched and unchurched, have benefitted from the services of Planned Parenthood in times of desperate need. Now, as Christians, we don't advocate for murder or killings, nor do we force people to make decisions that are not their own.

Jesus' defense of the woman caught in adultery is a powerful indictment of sexual injustice and manipulation. His stance challenges not only the misuse of the law to control and punish women but also any form of sexual exploitation and discrimination. This lesson calls us to stand against injustices that degrade human dignity and to work toward relationships and societies where sexuality is respected as a gift rather than weaponized as a tool of oppression.

Remember how Jesus' words caused the crowd to disperse? Their self-righteous façade crumbled when confronted with their hypocrisy. Jesus saw right through their manipulation and exposed the injustice women faced under the law. In today's digital age, it's common for people to jump on a public "shaming" bandwagon, calling others out for supposed moral failures or mistakes. However, when people reflect on their own lives, they often see similar struggles or mistakes, exposing their judgment as hypocritical. This moment of realization is like Jesus' words to the crowd, calling us to humility, introspection, and compassion rather than condemnation. May we also have the courage to see right through the façade of lawmakers and politicians who exploit the bodies of women for their selfish gain and power.

The Gem Being Dropped:

God desires justice for all His children, especially those who are vulnerable and exploited. He wants you to experience healthy, fulfilling relationships built on mutual respect and love.

TIME TO DROP YOUR OWN GEMS:

- How have your own experiences of shame or guilt around sexuality influenced your relationship with yourself and with God?

- In what ways can you practice discernment to protect yourself from those who might use spirituality to manipulate or exploit vulnerabilities, especially regarding sexuality?

- How can men create safer spaces for women and their sexual dignity so they don't feel scared, nervous, or exploited?

- Reflect on the notion that Jesus offers restoration rather than condemnation. How does this perspective shift your understanding of sexual mistakes and their impact on your spiritual life?

- How can you contribute to creating spaces within your community that uphold sexual dignity and justice, challenging both overt and subtle forms of sexual manipulation and injustice?

- What steps can you take to embrace your sexuality as a gift, integrating it into your spiritual journey in a way that feels healthy, holy, and healing?

- ♦ Have you ever encountered someone who used religion to control your sexuality? What was your response?
- ♦ How can you distinguish between healthy spiritual guidance and manipulation disguised as faith?

_____

_____

_____

_____

_____

_____

_____

_____

_____

_____

_____

_____

_____

22

THE GEM CROWN WE WEAR

As you turn the final pages of this book, I hope you feel the weight of these stories—not as burdens, but as jewels added to your crown. Each chapter, each woman, each lesson is a radiant gem polished by struggle, refined by resilience, and glowing with God's glory. Together, these stories create a crown that's uniquely yours, designed for you to wear boldly and unapologetically.

This book wasn't just about ancient women—it was about you. It was about reclaiming your story, your power, and your God-given identity. It was about hearing Eve whisper, "You are not your mistakes," or Esther boldly declaring, "Your beauty is an asset, not a liability." It was about seeing yourself through Sarah's laughter, Hagar's tears, Rahab's courage, and Tamar's justice.

These women are no longer just names in a book; they are now sisters in your journey, mentors in your struggles, and allies in your victories. They have shown us that life's complexities—our scars, our desires, our triumphs—are not obstacles to God's plan but integral parts of it.

So, what now?

Now, you rise. You walk into rooms with the confidence of a Queen of Sheba, carrying the wisdom of Ruth, the resilience of Hagar, and the strength of Bathsheba. You honor your body like the Shulamite woman, own your autonomy like Vashti, and pour yourself out like Hannah. These stories were never meant to be left on the page. They are meant to be lived—embodied—in every decision you make, every boundary you set, and every bold step you take.

God's heart for you is freedom. Freedom to love yourself, embrace your God-given beauty, and live authentically in your purpose. My prayer is that this book has given you the courage to shake off the chains of shame, step into your worth, and shine in the fullness of who God created you to be.

Because, sis, the world needs you—your voice, your light, your truth. There's a woman waiting to hear your testimony, a sister who needs to see what victory looks like when it's wrapped in grace and dripping with confidence.

Let this be your commissioning. Go live the gem-studded, Spirit-led life you were created for.

And when you need a reminder of who you are, just look back at these pages. Let the voices of our biblical sisters echo in your heart: "You are seen. You are worthy. You are enough."

Now go, Queen. Wear your crown.

GEM DECLARATIONS

Eve

- ◆ "I am not my mistakes; I am God's masterpiece in motion."
- ◆ "My vulnerability is my strength, and my story is worth telling."
- ◆ "I was made for deep connection and divine purpose."

Sarah

- ◆ "My age does not limit God's ability to bless me."
- ◆ "I laugh boldly in the face of impossible promises."
- ◆ "I am worthy of joy, pleasure, and divine surprises."

Hagar

- ◆ "The God who sees me calls me by name."
- ◆ "I am more than my body; I am a reflection of God's image."
- ◆ "Even in the wilderness, I am never abandoned."

Rebekah

- ◆ "My choices shape my destiny; I act with purpose and courage."
- ◆ "I carry the strength to navigate life's unexpected turns."
- ◆ "God uses my boldness for His plan."

Rachel and Leah

- ◆ "Comparison is the thief of joy; I celebrate my unique path."
- ◆ "God values me for who I am, not for what I produce."
- ◆ "Sisterhood thrives when we choose understanding over rivalry."

Tamar (Daughter-in-law of Judah)

- ◆ "I reclaim my worth, even when others try to deny it."
- ◆ "God brings justice through my resilience."
- ◆ "My boldness paves the way for restoration."

Potiphar's Wife

- ◆ "I confront the shadows within me to walk in integrity."
- ◆ "My desires do not define me; my choices do."
- ◆ "God calls me to transform my intentions into holiness."

Rahab

- ◆ "My past does not disqualify my future."
- ◆ "Faith transforms me into a woman of legacy."
- ◆ "I am bold, brave, and redeemed by grace."

Ruth and Naomi

- ◆ "Loyalty opens doors to unexpected blessings."
- ◆ "God provides abundantly through chosen family."
- ◆ "I am never without hope, even in seasons of loss."

Hannah

- ◆ "My prayers are powerful; God hears my every cry."
- ◆ "I trust in God's timing and faithfulness."
- ◆ "Through my pain, God births purpose."

Penninah

- ◆ "I release jealousy and embrace contentment."
- ◆ "God's blessings for others do not diminish my worth."
- ◆ "I choose grace over bitterness."

Bathsheba

- ◆ "God restores and redeems my story for His glory."
- ◆ "I rise from shame into a legacy of strength."
- ◆ "My worth is not defined by others' actions against me."

Tamar (Daughter of David)

- ◆ "I am not what happened to me; I am who God says I am."
- ◆ "Healing is my birthright, and I claim it boldly."
- ◆ "My voice matters; I speak my truth with courage."

Delilah

- ♦ "My power lies in my choices, and I choose wisdom."
- ♦ "I align my strength with integrity and purpose."
- ♦ "God's plans for me are greater than my missteps."

Vashti

- ♦ "My 'no' is a declaration of self-respect."
- ♦ "I refuse to be objectified; I am a queen in my own right."
- ♦ "Boundaries protect my dignity and honor my worth."

Esther

- ♦ "I am here for such a time as this."
- ♦ "My beauty is an asset; my courage is my crown."
- ♦ "I risk boldly for justice and deliverance."

Queen of Sheba

- ♦ "I walk into every room knowing my value."
- ♦ "Wisdom and wealth flow through me as gifts from God."
- ♦ "I command respect with my presence and my purpose."

Shulamite Woman

- ♦ "I celebrate love and intimacy as sacred gifts."
- ♦ "My desires are divine and unapologetic."
- ♦ "I embrace the beauty of mutual, passionate love."

Jezebel

◆ "I harness my influence with humility and grace."

◆ "My leadership thrives when it uplifts, not oppresses."

◆ "God transforms even the most misguided power into purpose."

Woman at the Well

◆ "My story is not over; God writes a new chapter."

◆ "I leave shame behind and walk boldly into grace."

◆ "I am a vessel of living water, pouring life into others."

Woman Caught in Adultery

◆ "I am not defined by my mistakes but by God's mercy."

◆ "I rise from judgment into grace-filled freedom."

◆ "God's love covers me completely and unconditionally."

BOOKS CITED

- Carr, D. (2003). The Erotic Word: Sexuality, Spirituality, and the Bible. Oxford University Press.

- Gafney, W. C. (2017). Womanist Midrash: A Reintroduction to the Women of the Torah and the Throne. Westminster John Knox Press.

- Gafney, W. C. (2020). Womanist Discourse. Westminster John Knox Press.

- Grant, J. (1989). White Women's Christ and Black Women's Jesus: Feminist Christology and Womanist Response. Scholars Press.

- Harris-Perry, M. (2011). Sister Citizen: Shame, Stereotypes, and Black Women in America. Yale University Press.

- Rose, T. (2003). Longing to Tell: Black Women Talk About Sexuality and Intimacy. Farrar, Straus, and Giroux.

- ◆ Trible, P. (1984). Texts of Terror: Literary-Feminist Readings of Biblical Narratives. Fortress Press.
- ◆ Weems, R. J. (1988). Just a Sister Away: A Womanist Vision of Women's Relationships in the Bible. LuraMedia.
- ◆ Williams, D. H. (1993). Sisters in the Wilderness: The Challenge of Womanist God-Talk. Orbis Books.

ABOUT THE AUTHOR

Pastor Kimberly Bulgin is a trailblazing faith leader, storyteller, and advocate for women's liberation. As the founder of The House of Women and creator of The S5 Lifestyle, she empowers women of faith to step boldly into their God-given brilliance by embracing spirituality, sensuality, and self-confidence.

An ordained pastor, sex educator, and survivor of religious and sexual trauma, Pastor Kim knows firsthand the power of breaking free from shame to reclaim your identity. Her journey from trauma to triumph has inspired women worldwide to rise above societal constraints, deepen their relationship with God, and embrace their divine power unapologetically.

Pastor Kim's ministry spans continents, from North America to Africa and the Caribbean, delivering captivating messages that dismantle oppressive narratives and spark transformation. She made history in 2021 as the first woman ordained in the Central States

Conference and Mid-American Union.

With over 15 years of experience as a preacher, musician, and resilience expert, Pastor Kim blends humor, biblical depth, and boldness to guide women on their journey of faith and freedom. Through her dynamic workshops, live events, and signature programs, she's leading a movement of women reclaiming their seats at God's table—not as silent followers but as radiant, fearless leaders.

Whether inspiring audiences with her music, unpacking the complexities of faith, or creating spaces for sisterhood and healing, Pastor Kim's message is clear: when women thrive, the world is transformed.

For more study resources, joining the House of Women community and so much more, connect with her at www. kimberlybulgin.com